QUALITY: THE BALL IN YOUR COURT

Frank C. Collins, Jr.
Rear Admiral, U.S. Navy (Ret)

ASQC Quality Press
American Society for Quality Control
310 West Wisconsin Avenue
Milwaukee, Wisconsin 53203

Published by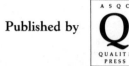

ASQC Quality Press
• Milwaukee •

Quality: The Ball in Your Court

Frank C. Collins, Jr.
Rear Admiral, U.S. Navy (Ret)

ISBN 0-87389-031-0

TABLE OF CONTENTS

FOREWORD

I have been reading essays of quality production for several years, and written a few myself. This book, by Frank Collins, is the best I have seen. But it rests on a mystery.

No American businessmen oppose this theme; none are opposed to turning out goods and services of high quality. Indeed, many believe they are doing so and have been doing so for quite some time.

Yet, with a few exceptions, most are simply not doing it. The telltale sign is our deficit in world trade, our national failure to compete in quality and price with the output of other nations. That deficit increases year by year. As I write, it has reached about $170 billion for the year, the biggest shortfall in trade ever registered by any nation in history.

It has meant that more and more of our industries are cutting wages, laying off workers, curtailing production, moving abroad — or simply giving up and closing shop altogether.

At first the decline affected basic industries, steel, autos, machine tools. Then the disappearance of American producers from consumer electronics, like TV sets and microwave ovens, became conspicuous. Now the hi-tech basics — semiconductors, those little memory chips, are going fast. It is ironic that, as I write, Fairchild, one of the two companies that invented the miraculous little chips, is under bid for purchase by a Japanese company.

It is sad to contemplate that if there were a world emergency, and we were called on to become the arsenal of democracy again, we probably could not do it.

The excuses generally given for our failure to compete have, one by one, been discredited:

> The value of the dollar rose too high in relation to other currencies, making our exports too expensive to sell, and imports from other nations so cheap that they flooded our markets and put our businesses, making the same things, out of business.

Well, at this writing the dollar has fallen radically for two years, and the deficits have gone on growing. Clearly the expensive dollar was an excuse, not a cause.

QUALITY: THE BALL IN YOUR COURT

Low wages gave the Japanese an advantage our high-wage businesses could not compete with.

I have on my desk a copy of *The Economist*, whose cover displays a large Japanese holding a small Uncle Sam in his palm, saying, "We are richer than you." The article inside states that unit labor costs in Japan now exceed those in the United States, and the average Japanese income has reached $17,000 to American's $16,000.

The Japanese beat us by resorting to unfair trade practices.

Well, the U.S. government has given special protections to industries that have made that assertion. Yet foreign cars take away more of the U.S. market every passing year. As this is written, General Motors — after pouring over $30 billion into automation and reorganization — has announced plans to close so many plants that another 10% of our market may be ceded to foreigners.

No, the truth has to be that our oral dedication to quality production is, again with a few exceptions, not being realized by action.

Why have we been failing in a field of endeavor in which we once excelled? I suggest that the principal reason is a psychological cycle that has become almost commonplace in American history. We have been an unusually successful nation. But our success has bred complacency and self-satisfaction.

Our last huge success was in not just winning World War II, but emerging from it with the only unbombed, undamaged, booming national economy left in the world. A wrecked world came to us to beg, borrow, or buy the means of survival. Such was the demand for American goods and services for about 30 years that our leaders — whether in politics or business — began to assume that U.S. economic superiority was part of the natural order of things.

There are a thousand illustrative examples. Typical of all was the visit in 1954 by Secretary of State John Foster Dulles to Premier Yoshida in Tokyo. Mr. Dulles told the Japanese Prime Minister — it was reported in every newspaper at the time — that Japan had best abandon the hope of finding markets in the United States. Japan simply did not know how to make things Americans wanted to buy. Japan, he said, must seek markets in the underdeveloped world. Well, we know what happened to that prophecy and that advice.

The hour is late for America to recover from our illusions and learn to compete. If you wish to understand the problem, and learn what to do, read on.

Howard K. Smith
Bethesda, Md.
January 1987

PROLOGUE

"Quality" is one of the most common cliches used in advertising nowadays. Whether you are buying hamburgers or mud guards, the buzz word is "quality." Quality is also one of today's most written about subjects, as a look through the newsstands or bookshelves will reveal. And quality is now the subject of more conferences, seminars, and special retreats than at any previous time in history.

Regrettably, neither advertising quality, nor writing about the subject, nor meeting to talk about the idea of quality alone will restore quality to American products and services. Should we conclude, then, that there is no way from here to there? Emphatically not!

There is a way to restore America to its traditional economic vitality by returning to the quality course that leads to job satisfaction, market competition, and economic advantage. To achieve this status, we must teach the right people — those who control resources — to understand their responsibilities and provide them with the "keys to quality."

Frank C. Collins, Jr.
Rear Admiral, U.S. Navy (Ret)
Alexandria, Va.
December 1986

QUALITY: THE BALL IN YOUR COURT

"When it is evening, ye say, It will be fair weather: for the sky is red. And in the morning, It will be foul weather to day: for the sky is red and lowring. O ye hypocrites, ye can discern the face of the sky; but can ye not discern the signs of the times?"

Matthew 16:2-3

INTRODUCTION

Japan has fascinated me since my first visit as a young Navy lieutenant operations officer on the Henry W. Tucker DDR 875 in November 1956. I've been an avid Japan watcher in the many subsequent visits I have made to that unique and beautiful island nation. I love the Japanese as a people and am intrigued by their industry and by their culture with its attention to detail. There is much we can learn from them.

During my '82 and '83 visits, my status as the executive director of quality assurance for the Defense Logistics Agency encouraged a great freedom of exchange, since I was an official visitor and not a competitor. I visited more than 30 industries and institutions and talked to countless individuals.

The following is a partial listing: Dr. Kaoru Ishikawa, president, Musashi Institute of Technology (Tokyo) and Dr. M. Imaizumi, also of MIT; Junji Noguchi, Union of Japanese Scientists and Engineers (JUSE); Kohei Goshi and Mikio Aoki, Japan Productivity Center; Fujitsu Corp. (Kawasaki plant); Yokogawa Hewlett-Packard (Hachiooji); Nissan Motors (Oppama and Murayama auto plants); Nissan Aeronautical and Space Division; Nippon Kokan K.K. (Keihin steel works); Komatsu (Tokyo, Kawasaki, Awazu, and Komatsu plants); Ministry of International Trade and Industry (MITI); Nikon (F3 and F3AF assembly plants); Toshiba (Fuchu plant); Fanuc (Fuji); Nippon Electric Co. (NEC) (Fuchu plant); Ishikawajima-Harima Heavy Industries (IHI) (Mizuko plant — Aerospace and Engines); IHI Tokyo Shipyard Division; Sanyo Shokai Ltd. (Tokyo); Kawasaki Heavy Industries (Gifu and Akashi); Yamazaki Mazak Corp. Ltd. (Oguchi-cho); Mazak Century 21 Automated Factory of the Future (Minokomo); Sony (Ichinomiya); Kyocera Ceramics (Shiga Gamoo); Kulicke and Soffa Ltd. (Tokyo); Sumitomo (Tokyo); Fuji Bank (Tokyo); Nitsuko (Shiroishi); Tokyo Juki Industrial Co. Ltd. (Ohtawara and Chofu City plants); Nomura Research Institute; and Yasuda Fire and Marine Insurance Co. Ltd. (Tokyo).

During my visit in 1982, I first noted the Japanese amusement about U.S. industry's curiosity about Japan's "quality secret." The Japanese candidly shared their "secret," generously crediting contributions by Deming, Juran, and Feigenbaum. Needless to say, not all of Japan's success can be traced to its ability to follow

QUALITY: THE BALL IN YOUR COURT

directions. In fact, during visits in 1982-83, I, along with my executive assistant, commander Ed Graham, and our American Japanese translator, Peggy Otsuka, determined that there were at least 40 factors that accounted for Japanese success in quality. After visits in 1984-85, I revised that figure upward to 60.

During 1982-84, I visited Europe on three different occasions to examine quality on the continent. My visits were limited to Citroen, Avions Marcel Dassault Brequet Aviation (three plants); Souriau and CIE; MAN; Zettelmeyer; MATRA; Aerospatial; Teleforban and Normalzeit; Battelle Institute; and Surveillance Industrielle de l'Armement (SIAR).

In 1983, I visited Korean industries and learned much about this awakening giant as I visited, among other, Oriental Precision Co. Ltd.; Hyosung Heavy Industries Ltd.; Gold Star Precision Co. Ltd.; KIA Industrial Co. Ltd.; Korean Standards Association — all of the foregoing in Seoul — and Korean Airlines (Pusan); Daewoo Shipbuilding and Heavy Machinery Ltd. (Okpo); Gold Star Precision Co. Ltd. (Gumi); Samsung Electronics (Kyunghi); Pohang Iron and Steel Co. Ltd. (Pohang); and Kukje Corp. (Pusan).

I had the privilege of visiting five of China's major industrial cities during a three-week tour in 1985. Beginning in Beijing and moving to Tianjin, Dalian, Shenyang, and finally to Quanzhou, we visited and spoke to many audiences and in many factories. Among them were Beijing Renmin Machinery Plant, #2 Chemical Works, Second Pharmaceutical Factory, Battery Factory, Shirt Factory, and Machine Works, respectively; Tianjin Radio Factory, Carpet Factory #3, and Orthopedic Instrument Factory respectively; Dalian Shipyard and Dalian Machinery Plant; Shenyang Heavy Machinery Plant and Heavy Machinery Plant Foundry; Quanzhou Electric Institute; and Far East Electric Fan Factory. We also spoke to large audiences at the International Club in Beijing, Tianjin Quality Control Association, Tianjin University, Quanzhou Labor Union Meeting Hall, and Jinan University.

This book was written to examine quality abroad and at home and to suggest courses of action to improve quality. These courses of action will be presented in lay language that every echelon of management can understand. They provide, in general and specific terms, the "how to" of changing the courses of economic history. The time for action is now.

ACKNOWLEDGMENT

Completion of this book has been a shared achievement for which I am indebted to many people. At the outset, I would like to recognize just a few of those who have made this book possible.

First, I would like to recognize the Bureau of Naval Personnel who posted me as its executive director, quality assurance, to the Defense Logistics Agency as my last flag assignment. What I accepted as a poor second choice to a cruiser destroyer flotilla command turned out to be one of the most absorbing, exciting, and challenging assignments in a 33-year span of such assignments.

This book is also dedicated to . . .

• All of my colleagues at DLA — and especially Col. Lloyd Gimple, USA (Ret), Ernie Ellis, and Bernie Mahar; the quality professionals in DLA-Q, Vice Admiral Eugene Grinstead, SC USN (Ret), my boss, and Don Moore, my deputy; Frank Carlucci and Paul Thayer, both former Deputy Secretaries of Defense and both of whom supported our Bottom-Line Conferences (BLC); Drs. Joseph Juran, A. V. "Val" Feigenbaum, Al Gunneson, and Stu Hunter, all of whom participated so effectively in these defense/industry quality dialogues; and to the scholarly dean of U.S. newsmen, Howard K. Smith, for the superb job he did of translating a day's BLC dialogue into a "pithy" anchorman's wash-up;

• Bob Bauman, chairman of Beecham Group P.L.C. and former chairman and CEO of Avco Corp., who determined that his legacy to Avco would be a quality culture and who brought me aboard to help him instrument it; Don Farrar, senior executive vice president of Textron and past president of Avco, for his unflagging support and participation in our quality improvement process for Avco; and to Avco's 11 major division presidents who cooperated in implementing individual quality improvement processes at their units;

• Ed Graham, who was my associate at Textron and was my executive assistant during my tour as chief naval advisor to CINC Imperial Iranian Navy and as executive director of DLA, for his wise and thoughtful counsel;

• My guides in Japan, Junko "Julie" Miyata and "Mike" Matsueda, and my interpreters, Noriko Hosoyamada and Kumiko Kato;

• My many Japanese, Korean, European, and Canadian friends and counselors in industry, including Dr. Kaoru Ishikawa, president of Musashi Institute of Technology; Dr. S. Inaba, president of Fanuc; Osamu Takahashi, Executive Managing Director of Komatsu Ltd.; "Terry," Tony, and Tom Yamazaki, Yamazaki Mazak Corp. — president, executive vice president, and senior vice president, respectively; Yuzo Kojima, general manager of Toshiba's Fuchu plant; Junji Noguchi, executive director of Japanese Union of Scientists and Engineers; K. Goshi, chairman emeritus, and Mioki Aoki, secretary general, Japan Productivity Center; Takeo Yamoka, president of Tokyo Juki Industrial Co. Ltd.; and Dr. Ryuji Fukuda, adviser to Japan Management Association and author of *Managerial Engineering* — all of whom provided me with insights into offshore quality;

• My 16,000 + DOD contractors, many of whom I was able to visit and dialogue with during my years at DLA;

• My reviewers and editor for their observations and suggestions;

• Peggy Thompson whose editorial advice I value highly;

• And, finally, to my dear wife, Esther, who supported me so faithfully on this project by being my chief adviser and typing most of the raw manuscript. Her biggest sacrifice was giving me up to the chore of writing this book on *her* time. To me, it was a labor of love and concern for this country; to Esther, a sacrifice of our scarce time together.

To all of you mentioned by name, and to the hundreds of unnamed friends and associates who have influenced me and given me input for this book, my sincere and heartfelt thanks.

CHAPTER 1

QUALITY: AMERICA'S DILEMMA

THE WORLD'S OLDEST PROFESSION

Many mistakenly believe prostitution is the world's oldest profession. Others, harking back to the garden scene, claim marketing (the serpent was having a sale on apples). Interestingly enough, neither sales nor prostitution (I guess both are in the marketing category) can claim to be first. Actually, the world's oldest documented profession is *quality*.

Genesis 1:31 gives us a widely accepted reference: ". . . and God looked at all that He had made, and it was very good. . . ."[1] *The essence of quality is described.* The conceptualizer, designer, builder, and marketeer of the universe did a first-article inspection and declared that it had turned out just as He had planned.

Another early source is the Code of Hammurabi, attributed to the Babylonian King whose reign — accepted as being 1728-1686 B.C. — marked the beginning of the first golden age of Babylon. His code, inscribed in an eight-foot high stele of black diorite, was discovered at Susa in 1902; it has numerous examples of the high esteem accorded quality workmanship.

"If a boatman caulked a boat for a seignior and did not do the boat well with the result that the boat has sprung a leak in the very year, since it has developed a defect, the boatman (builder) shall dismantle that boat and strengthen it at his own expense . . . ." (Article 234)[2]

Was this the first recorded warranty? Or, consider this persuasive motivation to do it right the first time:

"If a builder constructed a house but did not make his work strong with the result that the house which he built collapsed and so caused the death of the owner of the house, the builder shall be put to death." (Article 229)[3]

The Chinese appear to have institutionalized quality from the standpoint of government inspection as far back as the Ch'in dynasty: ". . . the penalty for poor quality ranged from a public lashing to fines and detonation of goods."[4]

1

TODAY'S PRIORITY

Quality is a priority concern in this country today. Perhaps more now than at any time in the past, the lack of quality in goods and services is having a serious impact economically in view of the market share and jobs we have already lost to foreign competitors through inattention to quality. The automotive, electronic, steel, shipbuilding, and appliances industries have seen the heaviest losses, with optics, clothing, textiles, and footwear coming in for substantial shares of the loss. Regrettably, it appears that the answer to foreign competition is for U.S. companies to have cars, engines, sewing machines, or TVs made by a foreign producer and marketed with a U.S. trade name. While this may make the product more competitive with foreign-label goods, it brings back not a single production job to our country.

This affects our balance of payments also. After years of being a nation of exporters — supplying not only raw materials but finished goods — we have become a nation that, according to Department of Commerce statistics, had an $83.9 billion trade deficit in the first half of 1986. Commerce further predicts that the total deficit in 1986 will reach $167.8 billion. This compares with $148.5 billion in '85, $123.3 billion in '84, and only $69.3 billion in '83.[5]

Impact on Military Readiness

From a standpoint of military readiness, quality is exacting an unacceptable toll. Paul Thayer, former Deputy Secretary of Defense, has called scrap rates of 10 to 30% a "surcharge" — an added cost that makes it more difficult for the Department of Defense to economize, particularly in the face of justified additional requirements. In addition, consider the effect on the morale of our troops when they see the poor performance of the M60 A-2 tank compared to the Soviet T-64. That morale problem is difficult to price out. Gen. P.X. Kelley, Assistant Commandant, USMC, in 1982 very succinctly summarized the issue of quality when he stated, "The failure of a weapon in combat doesn't just mean that you return it to the factory for repair. It normally means that someone will be killed. . . . I merely ask that you take a close look at the quality of your product . . . and recognize that its success or failure can well mean life or death on the battlefield."[6] Frank Carlucci, then Deputy Secretary of Defense, made the same point: "There can be no product recalls on the battlefield. No time for warranty work. The lives of American servicemen and women are on the line."[7]

It is hardly right for us to ask our military to keep the peace — with all the rigors, risks, and deprivations that charge represents — while we are unwilling to provide them with quality weapons and support systems.

INDUSTRY STATUS

To get an idea of the current status of quality, let's look at two key industry segments that have had wisely publicized quality problems: the automakers and defense contractors.

The Auto Industry

The U.S. automobile is perhaps the most easily recognized victim of the quality campaign waged by the Japanese. The proliferation of Toyota, Datsun (Nissan), Subaru, and Isuzu cars and trucks on U.S. highways is ample evidence of the success of their campaigns. A former Ford automotive executive candidly explained to me that, "We ignored the potential economic impact of the gas crunch of the early '70s. We didn't foresee that it would dissuade American car buyers from continuing their love affair with the luxurious gas hog, so we didn't develop more fuel-efficient models. We continued to produce and push the big car. We did it to ourselves," he sadly concluded.

The Japanese, standing in the wings with a compact car that was not only fuel efficient but also engineered and manufactured with a discriminating customer in mind, wooed the American buyer who was fed up with the built-in obsolescence of U.S. autos. This is likely to be a long and happy marriage. Quotas and tariffs will not dissuade Americans from buying cars that represent quality of workmanship and reliability, nor persuade them to buy U.S. automobiles marketed on the basis of $300 to $900 rebates and option gimmickry.

The auto industry has exacerbated the situation and lent credence to the myth that we cannot compete quality-wise with the Japanese culture by having components, and even total systems, built in Japan. But putting "Big Three" labels on what are essentially Japanese-built cars does nothing to regain jobs. The auto industry's current problem is management's indifference, not only to the customer and his desires, but also to what is going on down on the factory floor. Increasing return on investment and stockholder romancing have transcended the single most important responsibility of management: determining what the customer wants and satisfying that craving.

A major U.S. auto giant recently spent significant sums of money to hire the most prestigious prophets of quality to set them on a course to regain the American customer's favor. When asked what their priorities were, managers properly indicated quality as number one, ROI for stockholders as number two, and job satisfaction for workers as number three. It was suggested that swapping priorities number two and number three might be a more reasonable approach; with job satisfaction moved up to number two, stockholder's interests would be predictably achieved.

3

QUALITY: THE BALL IN YOUR COURT

While acknowledging the logic of such a suggestion, management was cautious about bumping the stockholder to number three in the list of company priorities. The stockholders' function of providing capital is essential; nevertheless, the product that provides ROI is made by the workers — from designers to mechanics at brand name dealerships. For too long now, the worker has been assumed to be important — but not to be *the* most important cog in manufacturing. The term "worker" includes not only the production worker, but also the designer, production and quality engineer, marketing and sales force, customer repair, and customer service personnel.

Defense Industry Impressions

Between 1981 and 1983, as executive director, quality assurance, Defense Logistics Agency, I had the opportunity to visit over 240 industries, running the product gamut from clothing and textiles to the space shuttle in plants located in the United States, Canada, Japan, Korea, Germany, and France. I was allowed to visit production lines, query the people on the machines, talk to quality personnel, and, most importantly, in most plants, speak to top management. Two hundred and five of my visits were to defense industries within the continental United States. Appendix A provides a breakdown of the visits.

My criteria in assessing the attitude and capacity for quality production contained some 15 to 20 factors. But, I honed in on six that are key to functional achievement of productivity enhancing quality. They are:

(1) Percent of plants with top management who appeared to understand the essence of quality;

(2) Percent of plants with effective systems for documenting scrap and rework costs;

(3) Percent of plants with effective formal training programs;

(4) Percent of plants with functioning quality circles;

(5) Percent of plants with aggressive automation and/or robotization systems or plans; and

(6) Percent of plants with effective systems for evaluating the effectiveness of a quality program.

My initial analysis — done after visiting some 175 plants during the latter part of 1981 through mid-1982 — indicated that in about 53% of the plants, management appeared to understand who was responsible for quality and how it was achieved. By contrast, some 88% of the managers spoke convincingly about quality in the last 86 plants visited from mid-'82 through mid-'83. This would seem to point to an upturn in defense quality, since quality depends on top management's perception of its importance and willingness to supply policy and resources needed to achieve quality.

4

QUALITY AFFECTS AND EFFECTS

Scrap and Rework

The picture was much less cheery in the "hidden factory" area. In the initial survey, only 15% had plans for documenting scrap and rework. Most recognized the need and were in the process of installing some kind of collection system. However, there also was a significant number who felt scrap and rework (S&R) was such a small item as to preclude the need to set up a collection system.

This reasoning misses the primary reason for documenting S&R — to correct problems. While the data will show the magnitude of problems (and, incidentally, should be compared to the cost of manufacturing rather than percentage of sales to emphasize the point more graphically to management, and, we hope, enlist aid in supporting quality with resources), the data can do far more by identifying *where* S&R is occurring. Follow-up can determine whether a deficiency is caused by lack of training, inadequate equipment, poor design, improper process control, failure to acquire best materials, poor vendor support, etc. By use of Pareto analysis — an analytical approach to looking at data that Juran has dubbed as the "vital few versus the trivial many" — management can decide what to attack and how much effort to assign. Without data, one has no accurate way of determining what needs to be done.

The hidden factory consists of much more than scrap and rework. Appendix B boils down the essential few and gives one formula for determining how effective the quality system you pay for really is. Unfortunately, not a single plant of the 243 had a totally satisfactory means of evaluating its quality system. The difficulty is obvious: the hidden factory adds additional cost in a great variety of areas. But trying to capture all of those costs would be self-defeating.

Training

There are as many perceptions of the need for and value of formal training as there are people being queried on this point. Few would admit that training is unnecessary in today's world of numerically controlled (NC) or computer numerically controlled (CNC) industrial machinery. Unfortunately, there are too many different opinions on how and how much is enough when training is the subject.

To be effective, training must be formalized, structured, and audited at regular intervals. The Edel-Brown Company, in Everett, Mass., serves as an example. This modest-sized machine shop has classrooms and a structured apprentice curriculum which ensures standards in training. Raymond Engineering, in Middletown,

QUALITY: THE BALL IN YOUR COURT

Conn., a producer of scientific and military recording devices, has an audit system which precludes workers getting out of certification or getting into production without proper qualifications. Too often, however, on-the-job training is considered adequate and, more often than not, the quality of such training leaves much to be desired. Of the 157 plants initially visited, only 25% had any semblance of a formal training program. Sixty-seven percent of the last group had implemented effective training plans.

The decline in the excellence of our education system over the past two decades has obviously affected quality. Inability to read or perform simple math computations sorely hinders understanding of manufacturing procedures.

Quality Circles

Perhaps the query which drew the most blank looks was the one on quality circles. "Oh, you mean that Japanese gimmick?" was the other reaction. Only 16.4% of the first group visited indicated that they had quality circles; regrettably, in most cases, few of those companies had any idea of what to expect or how to implement them effectively. Unfortunately, many circles died aborning. Obviously, the word about their value must have spread because 51% of the plants visited in the second group claimed to be utilizing quality circles to enhance quality.

Robots and Automation

While the United States has led the field in development of automation and robots, we have fallen behind in updating our industrial base with them. Only 17.6% of the first group had an aggressive automation/robotization plan. The excuses given: "We are waiting for the economy to improve," or "We need help from the government before we can improve our capability in that area."

It is not only simplistic, but futile to believe the economy will improve before we become more competitive quality-wise. Automation and robotics provide the ability to replicate a product at a competitive production rate. Both systems reduce the possibility of human error.

During my second group of visits, aggressive improvement in the area of robotics/automation could be found in 24% of the plants, a figure still much too low.

The Customer as a Quality Problem

Willis J. "Will" Willoughby, quality and reliability czar for the Navy's now defunct Material Command, sums up the customer's contribution to poor quality with one phrase: "We get what we accept." Without customer feedback, many producers blithely conclude that there is no problem. In other words, while the house burns, they fiddle because the smoke alarm hasn't alerted them to their situations.

Warranties give everything a false sense of security; they negatively affect both makers and users. Implying value and manufacturer's concern for the user, the warranty influences customers when they are deciding which product to buy. However, a combination of our national affluence — which makes replacement easier than the hassle of return — and lack of responsiveness of the warrantor renders most warranties totally ineffective as far as feedback to the producer is concerned.

How many times have you read the fine print on the guarantee or warranty, only to discover that it is cheaper to buy a new item than to pack up the old one and pay postage plus the handling charge? Let me give you a personal example. I recently purchased a new color TV manufactured by one of U.S. industry's most hallowed names. Within six months, a printed circuit board went bad. There would be no charge for the board, I discovered, but the installation would be $50.00 — even though, in my opinion, the manufacturer had a moral responsibility to repair the set without charge. It took me two letters and three phone calls before the maker finally agreed to reimburse me for the charge on the TV set. A less tenacious customer would have given up sooner. This game is also played by industry outside the United States. In light of the above, this seems harsh.

Customers' indifference to poor quality cannot be overlooked. If customers do not pursue their rights under the warranty, they will get what they deserve.

The issue of warranties has two sides: often, the customer abuses the terms of a warranty, causing the warrantor to become defensive. But, would it not be more profitable in the long run to risk an occasional rip-off by a dishonest customer than to fracture the loyalty of an honest customer by making it difficult, if not impossible, for him or her to get satisfaction? Consider Sears' policy of "customer satisfaction guaranteed." They've made it pay off by selling back defective merchandise to vendors — a valid and logical procedure.

When the government is the customer, it is in a unique position to influence quality. Unfortunately, that influence is often bad. We sometimes buy items that are beyond the state of the art in production technology. To compound the matter, we decide we cannot live another five years without this answer to all of our operational problems; as a result, we decree minimum development and production time. As must be readily apparent, when the time crunch is on, the first thing to suffer is quality. As a result, we live with an immature design or an inadequately supported system and blame failures on the manufacturer.

During one visit to the West Coast, I queried a general manager of a large industry about how he reacted to a "too-short" contract requirement. "We bring it to the procurement contract officer's attention." "And how does he react?" I asked. "He tells us, 'In that case, we would be unresponsive and may feel free not to bid.'" "And do you?" I asked naively. "Of course not. We bid. We have to survive," he answered without hesitation.

Quality's Impact on the Economy

Poor quality undermines productivity and contributes to inflationary pressures. Wage increases can only fuel inflation when they are not tied to increased productivity. As has been evident in the automobile industry, poor quality wipes out jobs as foreign competition causes buyers to seek a product made abroad. Few people who look objectively at the situation Detroit has made for itself will dispute the fact that many of the jobs lost to Japanese and European auto industries will never return to the United States. This is sad, particularly because it could have been prevented.

Poor quality further undermines our national reputation as a producer of top-notch goods. Most of us can remember the poor reputation Japanese products had. "Made in Japan" was the *sine qua non* of cheap and often times shoddy goods. Now, we can find a Japanese electronics firm rejecting up to 30% of the components shipped by its American parent — which, incidentally, may have a very high reputation for quality. Why? Because they did not meet Japanese standards.

Reputation is an intangible upon which it is difficult to place a price tag. Loss of it results, however, in a loss of market share and buyer confidence. Consider that a scant three decades ago the United States was a world leader in quality in automobiles and electronics, with Germany holding that title in optics and Switzerland in watches. Now, in all four, Japan is the acknowledged leader.

WHO'S AT FAULT?

Assessing fault is not nearly as simple as it might seem at first blush. It appears that we all have a piece of the action. Industry, as the producer, must accept a lion's share of the blame for poor quality. But, unions, the consumer, government, marketeers, lawyers, and design and production engineers all play significant roles in the issue of poor quality. Quality is a team effort that involves all hands. If we are to lick the poor quality issue in the United States during this decade, we must candidly evaluate the factors that contribute to poor quality and attack each one. We must not harken to the piper who says there is only one factor and one remedy to correct the situation. If the problem is not solved in this decade, it may well be too late.

CHAPTER 1: QUALITY: AMERICA'S DILEMMA

Perhaps the most difficult problem relating to quality today is a lack of understanding that quality is *not* just an acceptable product or service that comes off the end of an assembly line or from an office. Rather, quality must be a way of life, because achievement is the joint effort of the *producer* and *customer* alike.

Footnotes

1. *Holy Bible* (New York: Thomas Nelson, Inc., 1970), p. 1.

2. James B. Pritchard, ed., *Ancient Near-Eastern Texts Relating to the Old Testament* (Princeton: Princeton Univ. Press, 1950), pp. 163-180.

3. Ibid.

4. Ren Djou, "Historical Episodes About China's Quality Control of Weapons in Chou-Li-Kon Ge," *World Quality Congress Proceedings*, 1984, p. 179.

5. Robert Laird, "Our Growing Trade Deficit," *USA Today*, 30 July 1986, sec. 1, p. 1.

6. Speech by Gen. P.X. Kelley (USMC) at Bottom-Line Conference sponsored by Defense Logistics Agency, Washington, D.C., at Fort McNair, 13 May 1982.

7. Speech by Frank Carlucci at Bottom-Line Conference sponsored by Defense Logistics Agency, Washington, D.C., at Fort McNair, 13 May 1982.

QUALITY: THE BALL IN YOUR COURT

CHAPTER 2

QUALITY EXAMINED

QUALITY DEFINED

Trying to define quality can be described as being as frustrating as trying to tack Jello to the wall. Robert Pirsig, in his provocative novel, *Zen and the Art of Motorcycle Maintenance*, spends some 373 pages trying to define, describe, and explain how it is achieved.[1] In the *American Heritage Dictionary*, the number of lines defining quality is equalled by the number of lines giving synonyms.[2] "The essential character of something; nature" is its preferred definition, while "degree or grade of excellence" rates slot three.

Quality professionals use a variety of definitions. "Meeting the customer's expectations," "compliance with customer's specifications," and "fitness for use" are three popular and generally accepted ones. (See Appendix C for other definitions.) W. Edwards Deming, considered by many to be America's foremost authority on quality, offers this definition: "Good quality means a predictable degree of uniformity and dependability at low cost, with quality suited to the market." Maj. Gen. A.G. Rogers, USAF, former Deputy Chief of Staff/Logistics for the Tactical Air Command, has suggested that "quality translates technology into combat capability."[3] I believe that could easily be read as "quality translates technology into industrial strength or market leadership."

My own definition is, "Quality is profit to the maker, value to the user, and satisfaction to both." This means that Quality creates a "win-win" situation; it erases the "we-they" adversarial relationship that too often infiltrates the quality equation. In the final analysis, the customers define quality. They do this in two ways: by continuing their business relationships with you if they are satisfied with your understanding of their quality requirements; or by taking their business elsewhere, refusing to pay, or threatening suit if you don't make good. The latter three are fairly accurate indicators that your perception of quality does not coincide with your customers' perceptions.

Perhaps a good starting point is to take a moment to decide how you would define quality — as a top manager, as a line foreman, as an assembler, and then as a customer. Are there marked differences among the four perceptions? Probably so, and this, I believe, is the crux of our quality problem in America today.

QUALITY: THE BALL IN YOUR COURT

Top management, preoccupied with stockholders' interests, sees return on investment multiplying as production costs and time are reduced. Not replacing that tempering oven or not introducing NC or CNC or that new flexible machining center the MAZAK (Yamazaki MAZAK Co., Ltd.) salesman has been describing — all are means of cutting capital investments; the result is a stronger short-term bottom line, even if more and more of the product has to be bought off by a material review board. As long as the company can ship, that's what matters. Poor quality is shrewd business.

On the line, the foreman muses, "What exactly does management want of us? There's no published quality policy, and the production boss sounds like a Marine drill instructor with his constant move it, move it, move it. I guess as long as I can get it by the review board, I'm satisfying their requirements."

The electronic board assembler may reason, "Well, they haven't fired me, so I guess I'm doing okay."

The customer, of course, has other ideas: "Here comes my shipment from the Bare Minimum Co., late as usual and marginal, I'm sure. I've half a mind to return this shipment, pointing out how far off spec they are. But, since their shipment is late and I need those components to complete my production schedule, guess I'm stuck with them again.

"However, mmm — think I'll give Quality First, Inc. a call and see if they would be interested in supplying me. I've heard they concentrate on quality and schedule and are competitive in price also."

Far-fetched musings? Not really. Perhaps the proliferation of definitions has created the communications gap between design and production, between production and quality, between quality and top management, between company and customer.

Advertisers do little to clarify the situation. On the contrary, they appear to add confusion in their overuse of the word quality to sell products that can claim innovation only on the basis of styling intended to satisfy the jaded curiosity of a younger generation that has been surfeited by too much, too soon.

Trying to sell a poor product on the basis of quality merely causes greater confusion and cynicism on the part of the buying public. Leaf through a popular magazine and note how many ads have the word "quality" inserted to sell the product. Tonight, while you are watching TV, count the number of times the word quality is used and evaluate its appropriateness in describing the product. These overuses cause the whole meaning of quality to fade into a meaningless blur.

Quality is a Complex Term

From a user's standpoint, the concept of quality boils down to simple satisfaction with the appearance, performance, and reliability of the product — taking into account the price range you can afford. This doesn't mean you should have to buy a Rolls Royce or Mercedes in order to enjoy a quality car. Chevys, Fords, and Plymouths should also represent quality, i.e., satisfactory appearance, satisfactory performance, and advertised reliability. Our auto industry for too long now has focused on appearance and appointments and neglected consideration of engineering or production for performance or reliability. If you have ever tried to change the sparkplugs in a 1980 Chevette, you will know what I mean.

The first step in achieving quality is defining it as the customers do — comprehending the customers' desires. If there exists a gulf between what they think they have ordered and what you deliver, this is scored as a sure quality strikeout. A bit more time in market research or in studying the request for proposal or invitation to bid, and a thorough engineering analysis of the specs both by design and production to determine your capability to produce, may be worth millions in comeback suits or lost sales or follow-on contracts. The key here is communication and documentation. Know what your customers want and ensure that they know what you are going to deliver.

This is particularly important when you are bidding on a conceptual development contract. Often an eager marketer, anxious to sell a company's superiority, will suggest improvements neither stipulated in the concept proposal or within the firm's engineering capability to produce. Similarly, engineers — eager to press the state of the art — will improve the concept to the detriment of the desired system. The key, again, is to know what the customers want and give it to them.

Herein lies the edge Japanese and European manufacturers have gained.

Yuzo Kojimo, general manager of Toshiba Corporation's Fuchii plant, explained the involved process of interfacing between the customer, and Toshiba's design, manufacturing, and quality engineers *before* a new product is committed to production. This is the critical first step toward satisfying the customer.

The second step is equally critical: the transition from design to production. This may be one of America's most crucial pitfalls on the road to profitable production.

Design-Production Transition

The design-production hurdle plagues industry. While advanced technology affords design engineers great confidence in their ability to create almost anything they want, producing it is quite another thing. Why this roadblock? It appears hinged on the fact that these two events occur in widely separated worlds.

The design engineers work in a controlled environment. Their highly trained and motivated technicians can all read, write, reason, and understand the mathematics of engineering. The equipment used to make a prototype is, more often than not, state of the art, well maintained, and calibrated. Working conditions, while not always up to operating room standards, are invariably better than those on the shop floor. Achievement of test parameters with adjustment and fine tuning (the "tweak-and-peak twins") — a normal way of life with design engineers — assures success in that phase.

As we move to the plant floor, we hear, "Good grief! Do they actually expect me to build that gadget? Why, these tolerances are so tight we don't have a micrometer that can even measure that close. And these milling machines! Come on, you have to be kidding! And personnel!

"I've only got two men on the floor who would understand how to set up something like this. And the finish! Why, there's not a grinder in this plant than can produce what's been specified."

"Well, do the best you can, Joe, I have another project to get hot on."

And Joe does the best his experience, expertise, and equipment will permit, but it doesn't result in what the customer wanted — and was assured you could deliver.

On a trip to Japan, I asked two different companies how they handled this problem. Sadao Fujii, a quality engineer with Fujitsu Limited, confided that they assign some of their most promising young engineers to production for two to three years. During that period they receive a solid understanding of the real world of production. They understand that production-line workers seldom have the motivation or technical expertise of lab personnel. Conditions are far less controlled, and supervisor-worker communications often leave much to be desired.

The second firm, Ishikawa Jima-Harima Industries Co., has another practical approach. "We make the design engineers responsible for the product until it has achieved a cost-effective production level," says Kazuo Ishida, deputy general manager, aero-engine and space operations. This is certainly likely to cause some serious thought and to improve communications between the lab and production floor.

At least some U.S. firms seem to be catching on. At Texas Instruments' Trinity Mills Facility, one of the production group supervisors, when asked what he had done before his current assignment, confessed he had been in design. What has the experience taught him? "These things are one hell of a lot easier to design than to build." There is little doubt that, when he returns to design, he will be much better for the experience. Meanwhile, his time in production will be invaluable in product transition from design.

LOW OPINION OF WORKERS' CAPABILITIES

One of the greatest disappointments in visiting American industry is the low opinion management appears to have of the American workers' ability to compete with the Japanese in the realm of quality.

"Our people just can't ever achieve the success the Japanese have in the field of quality. The cultural differences, the Japanese proclivity for detail, and their acceptance of regimentation and group orientation give them an advantage with which we can't compete. The Japanese workers' respect for authority, their willingness to accept less for their labor, the lack of union interference. . . ."

It is true that the Japanese, in most cases, are culturally conditioned to be more attentive to detail. However, in studying the plan of Fujitsu's Institute of Management Training, one sees that this attention to detail is, for the most part, taught, not inherited. Flower and tea ceremonies, judo, and karate are all great detail disciplines.

The Japanese have unions — company unions rather than trade unions — but, nevertheless, bargaining units. As for ease of regimentation: Visit a U.S. Navy boot camp sometime and see how easily an off-the-street, "do-your-own-thing" dropout can be transformed into a spit-and-polish, precision-perfect example of enviable man- or womanhood. How is this achieved? Quite simply by requiring them to conform if they desire to continue. The same thing can be achieved with American workers in U.S. history.

Honda's Maryville, Pa., plant reinforces this conclusion. In this plant, where the production force and majority of supervisory force consist of U.S. men and women, the uniformed discipline equals that in Japanese plants — as does the quality standards. The Japanese general manager of the Maryville plant expects to exceed the quality achieved by Accords produced in his homeland, and it seems likely he will. Sony proved that this is possible when one line produced defect-free TVs for 200 continuous days in its San Diego plant. This record eclipses the best record Japanese workers have achieved.

So if cultural differences aren't the problem, what is? The problem is that management undersells American workers on what they *can* do or how *good* they really are. There are no finer workers in the world than our own American workers — once they are *told* what is expected of them. They are not *laissez-faire* workers. Left to their own desires and their independent natures, for the most part, they will do no more than a jumper you are training for a steeple chase. If you allow him to hurdle only those bars he easily clears on the first try, be assured he will never go any higher. Let him knock down the bars but keep urging him to try harder by raising the bars and, if he has the potential to excel, he will!

Union Considerations

Unions have contributed positively to the work force since their rise to power in our industrialized society, but, as Lord Acton so succinctly stated, "Power corrupts and absolute power corrupts absolutely." Today, unions often have a poor image among management and the public. This negative image is the result of occasional infiltration of our labor unions by criminal elements, plus the periodic rise to power of corrupt leaders (or corruption of those who have risen to power). Another reason has been an insistence on ever-increasing wages and fringe benefits, the costs for which are passed on to the consumer, who is stuck with a fixed income.

Nevertheless, the insistence by management that unions *per se* are responsible for poor quality is invalid. Unions have provided a unity of voice for the most important factor in manufacturing — the production force. The basic curse of U.S. trade unions is greed and a refusal to accept the basic economic premise that higher quality is the only path to increased productivity and improved competitiveness in the marketplace, and that these, in turn, are the only means of supporting higher reward.

Unions in Japan, recognizing these facts of life, have supported quality rather than assuming that the quality drive is just another ploy by management to increase profits by exploiting labor. In an interview in 1983 with Noriyuki Sugihara, elected head of the company union at Hewlett-Packard's Yokogawa plant in Hichioji-Shi, Japan, Suhihara explained, "We recognize that there are two approaches to improving labor's best interests. The first is to insist on a bigger share of the profits. This is valid to only a very limited degree. Since management supplies the capital, one of the two basic ingredients in production, they require and deserve a fair return on investment and effort. Repeated demands by labor for a larger share soon discourage investors and management alike and result in factory closure and job losses for labor. [Our steel and auto industries lend truth to this statement with the proliferation of silent plants now in evidence.]

"The second approach is to improve productivity. Automatically our share becomes larger. You see, we believe in the theory that, rather than demanding a larger slice of the pie, we all benefit when we work together to produce a larger pie."

This approach has worked in Japan, and it can work in the United States. In fact, recent concessions made both in the auto and transportation unions lead one to believe that the philosophy is already being acknowledged by our own union leadership.

Work Standards

What are your work standards? Have you established any? While some quality experts deny the need for quantified work standards, I believe they are valid. Taken in a vacuum, they are inadequate and destined to failure. But, taken in the context of factors we have already discussed, work standards not only set goals, but, additionally, convey to your most important resource — your people — what you expect of them.

Training as a Condition

Both chapters one and eleven deal with training, so I'll not go into detail here, except to say it is a critical factor in the quality equation. You *assume* the qualification of your production personnel at your own peril. Few people seeking employment will confess that they lack any skill you desire and, in periods of high unemployment, this is not unexpected. Desired skill levels are better assured by hiring untrained persons and teaching them your production methods. But to let them run amuck on your production line without training or company-oriented certification is akin to jumping off the Golden Gate Bridge under the delusion that you're lighter than air.

ZERO DEFECTS

What should the ultimate goal be? Zero defects — and nothing less. One of the great proponents of the zero-defect approach is Philip B. Crosby, chairman of the board and CEO of the Quality College. Crosby's philosophy is that you don't hire or pay people to make defective products or provide unsatisfactory services. If you agree, you use zero defects as a criterion for employment. Why not establish "make it right the first time" as a company production philosophy?

Doing it right the first time. How simple that sounds, and how logical. Why would anyone not want to do it right the first time? Who in management, production, or engineering would argue that point? And yet, 10 to 30% of defense production is nonproductive effort — scrap and rework.[4] And J.M. Juran, one of America's leading quality authorities, has observed that many U.S. industries have accepted a 15% scrap rate as normal.[5] Japan's scrap rate is 1%.

In 1979, when Thomas J. Murrin was president of the company's Public Systems unit, Westinghouse began a corporate-wide top-priority emphasis on productivity improvement — not a one-shot effort, but a "way-of-life" change throughout the corporation.[6] By seriously studying successful Japanese industries, Westinghouse learned that quality begets productivity. The company's goal was to improve productivity — based on annual increases in constant-dollar value added per employee — by 6% per year. In the first three years of that program, Public Systems, including its defense group, achieved a 7 + % annual productivity increase. Murrin said, "Now we're striving to get to 10% per year. A 7% improvement rate would double our output every 10 years, and a 10% rate would do this in about seven years."

The common complaint about zero defects as a quality policy is that it is unachievable. After all, as humans we are imperfect, and zero defects implies perfection. Here is what William F. Gibbs, designer of the SS America, has to say about perfection: "Perfection is an extremely hard taskmaster. . . . In the arts and sciences, it does not come easily. It comes hard. To get perfection, you have to demand perfection, and the people who demand perfection are rarely popular . . . and when it comes to perfection, I am implacable."

Man is imperfect, no question. But, if his goal in life or industry is less than perfection, he will achieve far less. Life should be a continuing search for improvement. This is what quality is all about: our search for excellence in our work and in our relationships with family and co-workers, all those aspects which we associate with quality of life. For those who feel any nation has cornered the market on effort or the work ethic, or who believe the United States should take a back seat to anyone in the area of initiative or innovation, I'd like to remind them of the special edge this nation of ours possesses.

We are uniquely blessed as a nation that has prided itself in being the melting pot. Our heterogeneous population is composed of people who, from the arrival of the Pilgrims, sought refuge in this land to escape oppression and avail themselves of the unlimited opportunities offered by this country rich in land and resources and having a temperate climate that allows people the freedom to excell. Even the convicts who settled Georgia emigrated to get that second chance. Today, our land welcomes refugees from the Middle East, Southeast Asia, South and Central America, Europe, the USSR, and Africa — people who are not afraid to work and contribute to the greatness of our society.

Regrettably, the media often finds it more newsworthy to focus on the sordid, rebellious, negative minority, whose only chance for immortality is to make headlines in protest or engage in irrational behavior. Fortunately, the majority of our nation consists of people willing, able, and ready to work, produce, and excel. They need only leadership and goals to galvanize them into a cohesive machine that won't accept failure.

It is my belief that management has failed to provide the caliber of leadership and guidance that considers the problems of unions, vendor control, and worker motivation as a challenge, instead of someone else's concern. If affluence has demotivated our working population, we need only to return to a policy of pay commensurate with productivity. We need to set goals and require accountability from all.

PROCESS CONTROL

Regrettably, during this period of exploding technology, we find quality control still using horse-and-buggy techniques. Specifically, many industries continue to pursue a quality control program based on final inspection.

What are the user benefits of final inspection as the essence of a quality control program? Printed circuit boards or integrated circuits that don't meet test criteria are tossed either into the scrap pile or are sent back for rework. Production chiefs in the semiconductor business report that, at times, scrap can tote up to 80% on new and exotic designs.

When defective product is scrapped, the entire investment — materials, labor, manufacturing facilities — is lost. The only possible advantage of this scrap is that, with a sound analysis program, it can pinpoint design deficiencies. Meanwhile, the rework pile will increase the cost of production by a factor of three: initial production; the rework effort that requires personalized repair and will, therefore, invariably require an effort greater than the original production line investment; and the product that will not be made due to the production effort required by rework.

At a modest transceiver assembly plant in southern Florida, 50 of the 250 people in assembly production were engaged in rework. The solution, simple and certainly not new, is process control. This approach analyzes the manufacturing process and determines where glitches are most likely to occur. Statistical process control represents a major contribution at this point, since it is both data factual and sensitive.

Who should be responsible for doing process control checks? I suggest it should be production personnel. Those who produce must accept the responsibility for the quality of their efforts and be held accountable for it. Quality personnel perform the invaluable contribution of auditing production's efforts, reviewing process control procedures, collecting and analyzing data, suggesting corrective action upon evaluation of failure analysis, and then, most importantly, following up to ensure corrective action has been taken.

The foregoing should not — repeat *not* — be interpreted to mean limited final inspection is unnecessary. First-article inspection is essential. This tells you if you have achieved your customers' desires and if the product fills your customers' needs. It is essential at this point to expeditiously implement any corrective action indicated. Thereafter, spot checks to assure that the process is still in control should be adequate.

Material and Component Availability

One of the characteristics of the American defense industry today is that very few, if any, of the larger prime contractors are anything more than integration and/or assembly plants. This introduces one of the really tough aspects of process control — vendor quality assurance.

And who is responsible for vendor quality? "Elementary," you may say. "The vendor, of course."

Wrong. Whose name goes on the end item — yours or the vendor's?

"Why mine, but. . . ."

No buts. The buyer gives not one hoot that ABC and XYZ supplied everything but the casing. They see the proud name of LMO on that assembled engine case and that's the name on the delivery invoice. Now who do you think is responsible?

Ultimately, the prime contractor is responsible. However, that company must never allow the vendor to take advantage of that fact by delegating the responsibility for quality to the prime. At one point in our country's history — the period during which we like to brag that "a man's word was as good as his bond" — certification by the vendor that the quality had been "built in" might have been taken at face value. Nowadays, the safest route is to act as if you're from Missouri and require objective evidence that the vendor can deliver quality on schedule.

Toyota has become famous for its "just-in-time" inventory delivery. Instead of having large warehouses for an extensive inventory with the attendant operating cost and capital investment, Toyota requires room for only two hours of inventory. At Sony's Ichinomiya plant, a Sony TV or Betamax VCR rolls off the line every six seconds. Does this require a large inventory of parts?

"No," says Kinnosuke Ikeda, manager, administrative affairs. "Every 90 minutes trucks from our vendors roll up and disgorge the components we need; we let them keep the inventory for us." But, of even greater importance, the vendors know that, in order for Sony to produce "made-right-the-first-time" TVs and VCRs, it needs quality parts. Moreover, the vendors' futures as Sony suppliers depend on their delivery of just that.

Yamazaki MAZAK Co., Ltd., in Oguchi, Niwa-Gun, has a unique approach to vendor control. When I visited Yamazaki in 1983, I noted a tote board laden with kanji-covered shingles hangs in a prominent spot in the receiving area. "That's our scoreboard," explained Kazuo Nishimura, international marketing manager. "To get on the top level, a vendor must have a 95% or better yield of no-defect delivery. And to get on the second level, he must have a 92% better."

There is no third level. "Vendors in the lower level are always competing for the top level, knowing that if Yamazaki has to cut back, the first to go will be the second-tier suppliers," Nishimura says. This makes the vendors compete for Yamazaki's business, with the winning edge being quality.

MARKETING CONSTRAINTS

How can marketing detract from quality? By overselling the product to the customer. The oversell can occur in slick brochuresmanship that describes or implies characteristics beyond the state of the art or beyond the firm's capability for manufacture.

A second oversell is the unrealistic delivery schedule. At times this may be at the insistence of the buyer — at other times, the suggestion of the marketeer anxious to beat out the competition. Be aware of the negative impact this has on quality in either case. In the first situation, the buyer may schedule a production line startup or new product introduction based on promised delivery date. This can lead to suits, countersuits, etc. Certainly it will lead to ill will and, in all probability, a lost customer. Where the described production capability does not exist, it can, at a minimum, raise doubts about the integrity of your sales force, and integrity is very much an issue in quality.

MANAGEMENT COMMITMENT

One of the most important elements of the complex makeup of quality is management commitment. It is important for two basic reasons. First, management sets the quality policy and, second, management controls the resources.

Quality Policy

It is dismaying to discover old-line, well-respected, state-of-the-art companies that either have no quality policy, or have established one only very recently. You establish a policy for working hours, sick leave, vacation pay, retirement, and incentive benefits, but quality has not been considered of sufficient importance, until recently, to require a published policy.

What should the policy say and to whom should it be disseminated? Appendix D has some samples, but basically it should be bikini-like in construction — brief enough to incite interest, but adequate to cover the pertinent aspects of how management feels about quality. There are policy statements that are as brief as two sentences and others that run six typewritten pages. The former is preferable. Too often, the latter give one the feeling that it is management's attempt to impress stockholders or customers. The policy really exists to explain concisely and understandably the degree of attention to quality that management desires and to assign responsibility for its achievement.

Take note: Once a quality policy is stated, don't try to short circuit it because certain customers want an early delivery and are willing to sign any kind of waiver to get it. This is a two-edged sword. Your workers will now know you have exceptions to the company quality policy, and the customers may only be willing to forgo quality until they take delivery and find that the product doesn't fulfill either their own or their customers' expectations. Military procurement personnel can cite numerous examples of the truth of this statement.

Resource Control

The second critical issue, which is solely the prerogative of top management in the area of quality, is control of resources: capital investment that will improve quality, expensive training effort, and creation of new areas of corporate expenditure — all decisions made by top management.

As Alvin Gunneson, CEO of the Gunneson Group, International, is wont to say, "I'm not interested in management support; I'm interested, as a quality manager, in participation!" This implies understanding of who is ultimately responsible for quality — (the CEO) — and how it is achieved — (the result of an all-hands effort).

Much of the problem in the area of quality today, I believe, stems from the lack of effective communication the quality community has been able to achieve with CEOs and COOs.

SIMPLY COMPLEX

What, then, is quality? It is a simple idea that becomes extremely complex when we try to put it in practice. Quality is as simple as the idea of making it right the first time, and as complex as the host of actions required to conceive, design, make, sell, and service any product.

In the final analysis, it is profit to the producer, value to the buyer, and satisfaction to both: profit to the producer because concentration on quality has raised productivity and thus a better return on investment and sustained competitive advantage; value to the buyer because the focus on quality has assured your customers that what they have purchased are products that will fit not only their needs, but provide them with the reliability that will keep them coming back, convinced you have *their* best interests in mind.

While this preoccupation with quality has a real-time payoff, of far greater value is the long-range ramification of top management's active participation in the enhancement of this nation's quality reputation and ability to compete domestically with imports and recapture foreign markets once ours. This, in the final analysis, is how our economic problems will be solved.

Footnotes

1. Robert M. Pirsig, *Zen and the Art of Motorcycle Maintenance* (New York: Bantam Books, 1974).
2. *American Heritage Dictionary*, 2nd College Edition (Boston: Houghton Mifflin, 1982), p. 1013.
3. Major General A.G. Rogers (USAF), "Product User," National Security Industrial Quality Conference, Hunt Valley, Md., 20 October 1982.
4. Speech by J.M. Juran at Bottom-Line Conference sponsored by Defense Logistics Agency, Washington, D.C., at Fort McNair, 13 May 1982.
5. Ibid.
6. Speech by Thomas J. Murrin at Bottom-Line Conference sponsored by Defense Logistics Agency, Washington, D.C., at Fort McNair, 13 May 1982.

QUALITY: THE BALL IN YOUR COURT

CHAPTER 3

WHO'S RESPONSIBLE?

OBSERVED MISCONCEPTIONS

Ask the senior person in almost any company who is responsible for quality in the company. Almost as if by reflex, the CEO, COO, general manager, or other senior manager will point to the quality manager. Among defense contractors, an alternative is to point at the Defense Contract Administration Service Quality Assurance Representative (DCASQAR). "That's interesting," you might respond. "In what section of production or design are they assigned? Are they a welder, lathe operator, engineer, draftsman, or what?"

"Why, in none of those places. That's my quality manager," will come the puzzled reply.

How can a quality manager possibly be responsible for quality when they don't make anything? With the possible exception of inspections, charts, statistical reports, and perhaps slogans, the entire quality function produces nothing.

A second answer, received on rare occasions, is "I am responsible for quality." This is a candid admission; and in the final analysis, the top dog is responsible for quality. However, as we will see in this chapter, quality is *not* a one-man show.

Some companies recognize that fact already. At a visit to Gould Defense Electronic Division in Glen Burnie, Md., I asked the question, "How many of you out there are in quality?" The unanimous unprompted response: "We all are." Gould employes made the point.

Top Management's Responsibilities

Attention to Detail. Top managers are not normally detail oriented. After all, they have grand plans to make and important decisions to consider. The worker bees can handle the details. Don't you believe that a top manager who is unfamiliar with the details of his business won't find himself stranded on a lee shore wondering what happened.

The late Admiral Hyman G. Rickover, USN (Ret), father of nuclear propulsion in the Navy and certainly a legend in his own lifetime, said this about detail *and* top

25

management: "The man in charge must concern himself with details. If *he* does not consider them important, neither will his subordinates. Most managers would rather focus on lofty policy issue matters. But, when details are ignored, the project fails. To maintain proper control, one must have simple and direct means to find out what is going on. There are many ways of doing this; all involve drudgery."

Rickover's words have a definite message for managers who aspire to success. Know what is going on and you will be much better prepared to plan, anticipate, act, and react as the situation dictates. By knowing what is going on, you can become master of your fate — "Captain of your ship," as it were.

Being Visible. This knowledge of what is going on must extend to knowing and showing concern for your people, and it must be concern that is more solid than words and fancy PR about how people-oriented the XYZ Company is. Demonstrate how people-oriented you are by visiting workers in the plant, cafeteria, and at company athletic events. Know your plants and people. Too much to ask? Too busy to get out and see what's going on? A glimpse of the president or chairman walking through the plant asking questions and showing interest has a value in boosted morale that no amount of money can buy.

"Why, he is a real person. Look how short/tall, handsome/homely, impressive/plain looking he is. He asked me my name. He asked me to explain what I was doing. He asked me how long I had been with the company and what I thought of working conditions. He shook hands with me." These are the spirit-boosting comments you will invariably hear when you take the trouble to get out to see and be seen by the people most responsible for your success as a CEO or COO.

Salesmanship. A successful top manager must also be a super salesman. It's obvious you had those qualities on the day you drove into corporate headquarters and parked in the slot marked "Chairman of the Board."

Now, however, you have reached a point where you must sell yourself not only to your superiors, but also to your peers and subordinates. Let's discuss the two new breeds of superiors you must sell: they are the board of directors — and you will get to know them intimately — and the stockholders, that faceless group who, at each year's stockholders' meeting, can ask all sorts of interesting and embarrassing questions. How are you going to answer their questions about deferred dividends or reverses in stock prices? U.S. management, in general, has done little to sell the idea of long-range growth and company stability for the future. Rather, preoccupation with short-term growth, acquisition, and significant ROI have been the yardstick by which CEOs and COOs are measured. This false philosophy will have to be altered if we are to survive in the international market.

Plant modernization, increased investment in research and development, and sounder wage and benefit guidelines based on production are the approaches that will cause the ship of industry to catch the freshening breeze of innovative management and long-range planning that will lift it out of the doldrums and put it on a competitive course for the market.

How do you sell this to a board of directors and stockholders? "The most challenging aspect of management," replies Gen. Shigeto Nagano, JSDF (Ret), executive vice president of Fujitsu System Integration Laboratories Ltd., "is to convince our stockholders that our management goals are to ensure a continued growth of their investment, and to provide a strength and stability for Fujitsu that will relieve them of concern about the future. It is not easy, but it is essential."[1]

Just as top management at times sells the U.S. worker short regarding its capabilities, we also sell the stockholders and directors short on their ability to understand and accept the logic of growth and stability vs. gimmickry and short-range gain. Needless to say, you must have a long-range plan that *produces*, or you will lose not only the stockholders' support of a long-range strategy, but your position as king of the corporate hill.

Corporate Expansion. Corporate subsumption of companies often leads the parent corporation into alien manufacturing fields. One might argue that, since the previous owners are present to provide continuity in management, there should not be a ripple in the new corporate configuration. This overlooks the degree of interest ownership normally provides *vis-a-vis* just being an employe, in whatever capacity. To have the responsibility for making major product-line decisions in areas of ignorance can often spell disaster. One must know the market for one's product line. The auto industry might be an example of management's ignorance or insensitivity to the market. It resulted in a Titanic-like disaster. Some may argue that knowing the product is unimportant at the top level — that knowledge of law or finance is more important. But consider the number of businesses going belly up during the '80s. It may well be that this epidemic is at least in part the predictable result of inadequate knowledge of market and quality.

Responsibilities of the Quality Manager

If quality managers (vice presidents, directors, etc.) are not responsible for quality, then what are they responsible for? Quality managers serve many important functions. They should, above all else, understand the process by which products are manufactured so that they can evaluate the potential effectiveness of proposed quality control procedures. This means that they should be a part of the design/development operation to help determine whether the product can survive the transition from lab to production line.

Quality managers should ensure that production engineers are part of this review. In coordination with the production boss, they should determine who will perform the in-process measurements. If production accepts this responsibility — which is

27

rightfully theirs — then the quality function should audit the results. Quality should also be responsible for collecting and analyzing data on quality improvement or deterioration, and publishing this information for management and workers in the design and production areas. As the result of statistical analysis, they should support the production boss in recommending new equipment or facilities to top management.

Evaluating, routing, and following up on failure analysis and corrective action should be key aspects of quality's job — it is the only way to prevent the same problems from arising again and again.

Customer product satisfaction must also be of prime concern to quality. This can be accomplished through personal interaction with customers, survey questionnaires, customer orientation conferences and tours, or other means.

Government Representative's Responsibility

If you are a defense contractor, you will probably have DCASQAR in your facilities, either as a resident, nonresident, or "DCASPRO." The resident is *just* that and may have significant staff, depending on plant and contract size and product complexity. If you are a smaller plant or are dealing with a smaller, less complex contract, it's more likely you'll work with a nonresident government representative. (Governmental nonresident quality people are assigned approximately three contractors each.) In either case, the quality representative will not only be responsible for quality assurance to your military or government customers, but may cover several other plants with defense contracts.

A very large plant with a high dollar value contract or high visibility product, such as the external fuel tank for the space shuttle, may be assigned a Defense Contract Administration Service Plant Representative Officer (DCASPRO). The DCASPRO includes contract administration, property disposal personnel, etc. In remote locations, often you may have an Officer-in-Charge organization, which is larger than a residency but smaller than a DCASPRO.

These people are responsible for the customers' best interests. The Purchasing or Procurement Contract Officer — for the Army, Navy, Air Force, Post Office, NASA, or the Department of Energy — writes or lets the contracts, but the Defense Contract Administration Service has full responsibility for administering them.

In addition, DCAS may be charged to do a pre-award survey to determine the capability of a contractor to fulfill the terms of the contract, not only from a facilities standpoint, but also from financial, management, and engineering standpoints. The Procurement Contract Officer does not have to accept this recommendation and, in a number of cases, either because of a paucity of bidders or a visceral hunch, the contract will be awarded contrary to the DCAS recommendation. In addition, DCAS may institute post-award conferences to ensure that contractors (particularly new ones) fully understand what is expected of them.

Administering a contract includes a close review to ensure that the contract clearly states what customers want and the level of quality for which they are willing to pay. The most stringent quality requirements are found in contracts for nuclear power propulsion plant system components. Level-one subsafe products are the next most stringent. MIL-Q-9858A is the most stringent nonspecial products requirement. It insists on complete documentation of the quality control system and a report on all elements that contribute to cost of quality — an onerous and misleading label, since the cost is really caused by nonconformance, not quality data.

Another standard, MIL-I-45208A, is less demanding. It implicitly relies more on inspection than process control. Less demanding still is standard Form 32, which assumes QC to be the responsibility of the contractor. As a result, there is no formalized procedure specified in the contract.

The DCASQAR is responsible for reviewing the contractor's quality control system to see if it will meet the customer's quality desires. First-article inspection, if called for by contract, spot checks to ensure the quality process is controlled, and end-item spot checks supplement the front end verification of vendor components or base materials. The representative's signature does three things: It confirms acceptability of material to contractor, signals the paying office to write a check, and assures the customer that the product is as specified in the contract.

As is readily apparent, the DCASQAR, while not responsible for quality, is responsible for seeing that products failing to meet customer specs are not shipped. A key person in the quality equation, the QAR must never be intimidated by contractor or customer.

There is always the possibility of intimidation by contractors who have a quality or cash flow problem, or who feel that mil specs are not binding on a company that successfully supplies similar products to the private sector. Customers can also be very intimidating when pushed by schedule or budget windows, and may press the QAR to accept the end item on waivers. If the product was initially overspecified and performs satisfactorily despite noncompliance, the contractor and the quality representative may escape unscathed. But if the product bombs, as has occurred in the past (and particularly if it draws media attention), the QAR and the contractor who waived specs may be in for a pounding.

Waivers and Material Review Board actions are both signals that specifications have not been met and, although the customer may approve discrepancy, you ship with the risk of customer dissatisfaction. If the customer is genuinely happy, you should consider an engineering change proposal to bring the specs into accord with the new standard you have inadvertently created.

Failure to heed QAR counsel concerning procedure or product quality may inspire the QAR to activate corrective action methods ranging from a verbal suggestion to withdrawal of the DCAS rep's product quality assurance activities in your plant. Then, unless your customer will accept your product without a QAR signature indicating satisfactory quality assurance, you may suddenly come down with a severe case of cash flow anemia. The QAR may also call out the quality problems you are having and advise the customer to investigate.

Government reps should be considered members of the quality team that is looking out for the best interests of the contractor — a means of enabling them to continue delivering products to customers who do not normally experience the economic fluctuations of the private sector. They also consider the interests of taxpayers, who are increasingly burdened by deeper incursions into their incomes. QARs must be allowed to be objective outsiders, who enjoy nonadversarial relationships — if they are to be able to help you with your quality problems and keep your relationships with customers on an even keel.

Prime's Quality Rep

If you are a subcontractor, as most manufacturers now are with the trend toward specialization, you may have a prime contractor quality rep assigned. The representative's function is to look after you and the prime's best interests. To get rid of the rep, you will have to hone your manufacturing system to the fine point of being able to consistently ship defect-free products to the rep's employer. At that point, the prime will have no alternative but to back the company's rep out of your plant, since that rep has obviously become an unnecessary expense for the company.

Production's Responsibility

The lion's share of responsibility for quality occurs on the production line, but an "undo-able" design can doom quality, as can equipment incapable of holding required tolerances. Purchasing inferior materials or components can also impact production. The low bidder whose bid is based on poor quality can turn out to be the biggest drain on profits or the main cause of cost overruns.

The shipping department, too, can thwart production's best attempts to produce a quality product by damaging the finish, by causing misalignment, by poor packaging, or by just not following customer's contract instructions. If the customer, for instance, has specified one valve per box and shipping packs two, quality has not been delivered. Customers can seem unreasonably demanding at times, but, remember, they are your *raison d'être*.[2] While it is perfectly logical for the government to want to be good stewards of public funds, low bid is not necessarily the way. Often, unqualified manufacturers or even brokers who have no facilities will bid a job low and then shop for someone to build it for them. This means that, in order for either to survive, they have to pare everything to the bone. Normally, this will include quality, and you end up with junk. No Procurement Contract Officer knowingly awards a contract to an unqualified bidder, but sometimes there is insufficient time to investigate; sometimes political pressures are brought to bear. In such cases, the quality system takes the crunch.

WHEN EVERYONE'S RESPONSIBLE, IS ANYONE RESPONSIBLE?

If everyone has a piece of the quality pie, on whom do you pin the tail when quality sours? President Truman's oft-quoted desk sign, "The Buck Stops Here," has been misinterpreted to mean that no one below the top has sufficient responsibility to be held accountable. That kind of thinking can be disastrous. If a general manager, through lack of attention to detail and counsel, steers the corporation into an *in extremis* situation, he should be canned — not transferred to corporate headquarters to cool off or retire gracefully. If the production chief cannot produce a quality product despite a debugged design and on-spec materials, then the production chief — not the quality chief — should be pink slipped. If the maintenance personnel cannot maintain equipment and the custodial division cannot keep the working area free of debris, replacement is reasonable. These removals should not be done without counseling or warning, but all parties must recognize that the concept of accountability includes this unpleasant repercussion. A *laissez-faire* approach to accountability in both the private and public sectors has created the illusion that there is no accountability for anything up to and including murder in our society.

Blue vs. White Collar

Deming attributes the bulk of quality errors to the system, and the system belongs to management.[3] Why then is it so popular to beat up on the blue-collar work force? Probably because white-collar workers are more adroit at passing the buck down than blue collar workers are at passing it up. If the product is out of tolerance, it would be fairly easy to trace down the errant artificer who has a controlling contribution to that process.

Design has remained aloof and remote from the area where the chips and sparks fall. Designers often consider their responsibility ended once the design has been committed to hard copy. Similarly, management has always excused environments that mitigate against quality.

"Automation? Too expensive and business too slow. Update of machinery? No. The board of directors will never sanction it. Training? I learned my trade through on-the-job training. Insufficient time to develop and produce? Okay, design and production, work it out. We need this contract. Have quality report directly to the general manager? Why, if I do that, the next thing I know, the manager will be wanting more money." Those responses can devastate a quality program.

QUALITY: THE BALL IN YOUR COURT

Marketing's attitude problems sound like this: "Visit a customer to see if he's satisfied with our product? Look, I have too much to do trying to sell our product. I can't spend time checking to see if anyone has any problems."

Or, "If we tell the customer we can't deliver in that time frame, we'll lose him. Besides, he's not too fussy when we're late." Or, "I thought you (production) guys could do anything. I told the customer we could improve on his specs."

Deming's identification of white collars as the main cause of quality problems is due to their responsibility for all the significant decisions regarding resources, facilities, and engineering. To exempt these elements from accountability for quality is indeed mindless management.

When we speak of management (those mysterious forces who always seem to be pitted against our best interests), who do we mean? For our purposes, management is anyone who has authority to allocate or withhold resources and make policy decisions. These two factors identify management as the most important factor in industry's side of the house as far as quality is concerned.

Loyalty

Loyalty, for the most part, has become rather passe in today's work-a-day world. People do not identify with the LMO Company to the degree they once did. This is because, in our mobile lay-off, recall-oriented industrial world, workers move from one job to another as the opportunity presents itself. Japanese management marvels at our ability to exact *any* loyalty with on-off hiring policies dictated by market demand and economy.

The adversary relationship that has characterized management-labor relations for so many years is another area that discourages company identity and loyalty, and that, in turn, does nothing to increase dedication to higher quality.

Recent actions on the part of the rank-and-file workers (voting unions out of plants or opposing their formation) demonstrate that workers are beginning to demand a greater concern for their best interests from union leaders. Arbitrary rejection of company wage packages, when the logic of the computation of the proposals is obvious, has aroused a tide of worker resentment as well as public sentiment against the unions' self-serving leadership. Conversely, failure of management to keep faith with labor after such a concession has been made by awarding top management huge bonuses can be disastrous.

Recall the time when it was considered that the workers *were* the company. The return of such a feeling of identity and unity of purpose will have a salutary effect on quality, and the return of this identity factor is dependent on union leadership and corporate management that can demonstrate that they have the workers' best interests at heart. Lifetime employment, willingness to compromise to promote the best interests of all concerned, willingness to go that second mile, implementation of quality circles (discussed in a later chapter) — all these will convince workers that they are truly a part of the LMO Company and that their own interests are best served by quality work that enhances productivity and permits them to *earn* what they are being paid.

THE CUSTOMER'S ROLE

The customer, too, plays a vital role in the quality of the delivered product. His role begins with the writing of the contract. The contract should not leave much to a contractor's imagination. It is *insufficient* for the customer to know what he wants. He must also *communicate* his desires to the contractor.

Nor should specs of related items be scattered throughout the contract. Some customers feel that, if a spec is in there, it's the contractor's responsibility to ferret it out and comply. In contrast, the customer who is really interested in quality will work to eliminate anything that may give the contractor problems.

A case in point: A customer's receiving department was complaining that 99% of the products received were not packaged correctly. What could possibly account for that remarkable level of nonconformance? The desired packaging was specified in the contract, but bureaucratese and legalese had so garbled the instructions that it took a professional contracting officer a couple of hours to unscramble it. Consider the poor "bicycle shop," with limited talent, trying to piece it all together. Legally, the customer in this case was clear, but the unclear specs were tantamount to no specs when it came to assuring the desired quality.

Even the U.S. Navy can be, at times, a customer that places unreasonable demands on contractors. Concerned with keeping ahead of our military foes, the Navy understandably wants the latest technology has to offer, and they want it today. A senior military spokesman, a fleet commander, put it this way: "The Navy should be more patient in not insisting on production of a weapon before it is mature. We need a working, reliable system when it gets there."[4] As the saying in Washington goes, "If you want it bad, you get it bad."

Standardized Contract Form

Another way in which the customer hinders quality and distresses contractors is by using nonstandard contract forms. This is particularly true of military contracts. Each service — yes, each Procurement Contract Office — may have its own contract format. To a small contractor with limited legal expertise and limited staff, this can pose a problem. It becomes difficult to determine whether all the wheat in a chaff-filled contract has been successfully gleaned.

Part of the problem is the varying degree of expertise and experience that government quality assurance representatives possess. Fortunately, many of their basic training courses have recently been revised, and several new courses (covering additional subjects) have been instituted. As more QARs complete these courses, inspection — and contracts — should become more standardized.

Performance Expectations

When specs call for precise tolerance or documentation and then these specs are waived in order to get delivery, the contractor questions whether the customers really know what they want. The contractor wonders the same thing when the customers specify an item that is clearly beyond the state of the art. "But unless we push the state of the art, we will never know what is possible," you might argue. In basic research or research and development projects that may be true but, when the item in question is truly meant to be produced and delivered to a consumer with immediate needs, realism — not reaching — is what specs should reflect.

The point here is for the customer: If you are interested in quality, spell out what you want and then demand it. If it's impossible to produce, acknowledge this and reduce the spec, but avoid waivers. They *desensitize* the contractor and make a mockery of your real needs.

Much customer-contractor confusion can be eliminated by improved communications. Candid admission of confusion early on may save a heap of embarrassment later. Is it better to be thought dull or found stupid?

THE FOUNDATION

But where is the first brick, rebar, and mortar of quality laid? I suggest it's in the home. Parents who lack the foresight or intellect to teach children responsibility for their actions, those who fail to follow up when children disobey or fail to complete assigned tasks (chores or school work), are planting the seeds of nonconformance. This is where phrases and attitudes like "good enough" or "good enough for government work" are conceived. The foundations of character are "poured" in the home. Schools, at times, can correct poor foundations, but don't count on it. If you question some other institutions' concern about your progeny's character, ensure that you take the time to do the foundation work yourself.

And what does this foundation laying have to do with quality? Almost everything. It's exemplified by parents who are interested enough in their children's futures to commend them for a job well done and counsel them on poor effort. It's a constant example of best effort by parents and relatives in all that they do. It's honesty lived in the home. It's personal habits of hanging up clothes, putting away tools, and keeping the house clean. Trivial as all this may seem, it sets the background for habits that, later in life, will identify and separate a quality-oriented person from one whose basic training has taught him to believe that getting by is adequate and that the 110% philosophy of former Redskins' football coach George Allen is pure eyewash.

Just as quality is the product of a number of people, so is nonconformance. Developing a quality worker is a lifelong process; reorienting a worker who has never been taught or forced to care, is no overnight task, regardless of the method used. But, bear in mind, identification and understanding of the problem are the first giant steps toward correcting them.

Academe

Ever since publication of the presidential panel's study on the quality of education in the United States, *A Nation at Risk*, 1983,[5] America has become acutely aware of the fact that education in this country has been far from successful. Can we conclude that this situation has affected quality?

Most in the quality community would vote a resounding "Yes!" Education is the second rung in the development of a quality philosophy. It is in this environment that our future managers, engineers, computer programmers, lathe and machine operators learn to read and reason, multiply, divide, and understand equations and statistics. This is in primary and secondary schools.

In college, they learn how to think and reach decisions using a logical thought process. Regrettably, it appears we missed the boat at the readin', writin', and 'rithmetic stage. There is no way a person can be a quality craftsman if he cannot read blueprints and machinery procedures — not in today's complex technology.

In addition to failing in the basics, many schools have failed in the philosophical area — where students learn the basic "Rs" of responsibility — first, the essentials of responsibility and, second, who is responsible for what.

The failure of business schools to emphasize top management's role in the quality equation is also quite disquieting. So is the number of engineering schools that focus their quality curricula on inspection of techniques rather than on process control. It is hoped that the Defense Logistics Agency's Bottom-Line Conferences in April of 1983 and '84 have sparked academe to consider a significant curriculum revision.

COST OF CHANGE

The Navy, over the past few years, has taken a great deal of heat over its significant cost overruns. To the uninitiated, these overruns seem unreasonable. Many, however, are not unreasonable at all, but are caused by our rapidly changing

technology. Failure to take advantage of technological changes would be impru-
dent, but the contractor will hardly feel inclined to give the customer a bargain
price for changes that interrupt his schedule. Hence, the Navy pays through the
nose. Cost overruns caused by these product improvements are not the problem.
The problems are the engineering changes that occur as a result of the customer
not having provided proper specs. One contractor reports that a certain customer
gave him *over* 5,000 changes/corrections during production. That is inexcusable.
Customers aren't alone in their culpability on changes. Contractors' design sections
are probably equally guilty.

How does an engineering change impact quality? Once production has begun, if
the change is significant, it requires "reproving" the line from a quality standpoint.
It also raises questions in production as to the capabilities of design engineering.

Government-Furnished Equipment

With the rapid growth of technology in both product and production machinery, it
is often difficult for a producer to acquire quality production equipment,
particularly if it is operating on a slim profit margin. It is therefore not unusual for
the military to underwrite the cost of new equipment (which is then designated
"government-furnished equipment"). The customer will benefit in quality and
schedule from such an investment. Expecting too much from old equipment can be
more costly, in the end, than replacement.

Footnotes

1. Interview with Shigeto Nagano, Executive Vice President, Fujitsu System
Integration Laboratories Ltd., Tokyo, Japan, 1982.
2. Translated: reason for being.
3. W. Edwards Deming, *Quality, Productivity, and Competitive Position*
(Cambridge, Mass.: Massachusetts Inst. of Technology, 1982), p. 68.
4. Remarks by Adm. Sylvester R. Foley, Jr. (USN) at Bottom-Line Conference
sponsored by Defense Logistics Agency, Washington, D.C., at Fort McNair, 1 June
1983.
5. *A Nation at Risk*, National Commission on Education Excellence (President
Ronald Reagan's Blue-Ribbon Panel) issued 26 April 1983.

CHAPTER 4

COMMON MISCONCEPTIONS

There are many common misconceptions that relate to management, the relationship of government and industry, culture, prosperity, affluence, and mobility — all of which affect quality. In warfare, the basic principle of victory is to know your enemy. In the case of quality, anything which inhibits its achievement is to be considered the enemy.

KNOWING THE ENEMY

Updating Facilities

"Can do" is a wonderful characteristic. The Sea Bees used it to good advantage during World War II as they carved bases out of steaming jungles and harbors from coral-rimmed beaches in the South Pacific. "Make do" is quite another thing. Many plants make do with outdated, outmoded, and, in some cases, only marginally operative equipment and facilities. This may be because plant management intends to wait for "better times" to make a capital investment that should have been made ages ago.

Putting off modernization until you can afford it is somewhat like putting off marriage or family for the same reason. In most cases, marriage makes life richer and fuller and, when you finally take the plunge, you wonder why you waited. So it is with modernizing a plant. It requires faith in the future. What, during this nuclear age, doesn't? It also requires confidence that modernization will improve productivity through quality and that the latter will improve your reputation of being a contractor who can deliver quality products on time, within budget.

The Defense Department has an inventory of outdated machinery at the Defense Industrial Plant Equipment Center. The equipment dates from World War II and the Korean War and, since contractors can use this machinery on Defense contracts by paying only a refurbishing charge (if it is necessary), many avail themselves of it. This equipment was adequate in its day, but, unlike French wine, it does not get better with age.

Usually, you can draw a direct correlation between equipment and quality. In some few cases, people make the difference. Their dedication and skill enable them to make silk purses with sows' ears, but in most cases the product falls short.

QUALITY: THE BALL IN YOUR COURT

Government Aid

Because several industrial giants have been revived by government bail outs, there is a popular misconception that government aid will restore vitality to U.S. industry. As the old adage goes, "There are three classes of people: those who watch things happen, those who make things happen, and those who wonder what happened." Those who wait for the U.S. government to rescue them will wonder what happened when they go under.

Just what is the government's responsibility to business and commerce? It is to provide a free society in which business can compete, grow, succeed, and expand to international markets. Do we want it to play a bigger role? Are you ready for more government red tape, regulations, and intervention? If you want government financing, you can count on giving up a degree of independence and freedom in management. Already we are engulfed in a sea of paper which, in and of itself, causes entrepreneurs to throw in the towel.

Maintenance of a free society in which people are able to work, express themselves, and live in a reasonable degree of security is primarily what we in industry should expect from government. We should expect our tax dollars to keep the sea lanes open for commerce and promote mutual trade relations in the international marketplace. But Santa Claus, Uncle Sam *ain't*.

Political connections may promote largess from the public coffers, but they don't solve the management problems that caused the need. Government subsidies to industry weaken initiative, the impulse to innovate, and ingenuity of management to operate in a competitive arena, and it creates a need for continued support.

It should be remembered that governments have no source of money except from the people they govern. Government is a nonproducing but significant consumer of public productivity. To the extent that it provides us a free and just society with free market opportunities, it is worth the price, but subsidies create the *appearance* of supporting employment and commerce. In the final analysis, they can sound the death knell to any industry that depends on them. Our Merchant Marine is a classic example of wages outpacing productivity and encouraging noncompetitiveness. Many will argue that the Soviet Union and other European and Far Eastern nations keep their merchant fleets alive with subsidy. This is true, and to the extent that our merchant fleet is an auxiliary of our Navy, our subsidies may be justified. But, in general, subsidies ensure that a business will never be self-supportive or competitive.

Protective Tariffs

The protective-tariff game is a vicious cycle that ultimately creates a lose-lose situation. It makes regulated trade in foreign markets almost impossible. It places an artificial barrier to peace by precluding free travel and cultural exchange that help us to know our neighbors. It's a game that admits that the other fellow can do something better or cheaper than we can.

Instead of putting up a fence, why not examine why our neighbor excels? This is precisely what the Japanese did, with General MacArthur's urging and assistance. They examined the reasons U.S. goods were considered desirable while their own were considered "cheap junk."

Learning quickly and foregoing pride (so expensive to maintain), they adopted our methods of statistical quality control, automation, etc., and presently are outdoing us at our own game. Slapping a tariff or quota on Japanese cars is not the way to take care of the problem. Possibly, not even joint ventures (GMC-Toyota, etc.) are the answer, unless we are willing to admit that they are better designers or are superior in production or management methods.

UNDERSTANDING THE COMPETITION

For a number of years, many in management have underestimated either the potential or the perseverance of the Japanese as industrial competitors. "Yes, they got in there with their compact Toyota and Honda and Datsun and cut into our sales a bit. But don't worry — we've always had the American buyer in our pocket. He'll come running back when we whistle," they say (spoken in the manner of an elephant indifferently considering a fly on the toenail of its left front foot).

But the American sports car buyer, we have discovered, enjoys the feel and responsiveness of the Datsun 280Z and its successors; American families appreciate the solid, compact lines of the Honda Accord; and there's American appeal in the Nissan pickup's living room quality stereo and solid, nonrattling body.

Until and unless the Japanese begin to ignore quality in manufacturing or service, few Americans will go back to their old buying habits. Complacent U.S. manufacturers are sleeping through the business equivalent of Pearl Harbor. Their sleep is encouraged by horror stories of how shaky the Japanese economy is and how affluence is changing the appetites and attitudes of the Japanese. These stories create an illusion that competition will soon pass.

Those who wait for the Japanese to fall off the horse through their own clumsiness may wait quite a while. Reacquisition of a solid quality work philosophy in the U.S. is much more likely to unseat the Japanese.

Korea is also waiting in the wings to come center stage if and when the Japanese price themselves out of the market. The Koreans share the Japanese view that customers deserve quality and they enjoy the advantage (over Japanese and American producers) of a low cost of labor.

QUALITY: THE BALL IN YOUR COURT

Cultural Differences

Also, wishful thinking is the citation of cultural differences as the reason we're unable to compete with the Japanese. Granted, there are cultural differences between our work force and theirs.

Take the preparation and service of food. To eat in a Japanese restaurant in Japan is not just nourishment — it is an experience. The care with which each vegetable and meat or fish entree is prepared is not unlike an artistic performance. There is more attention and care devoted to the production of a sandwich in the deli of a Japanese department store than there is at most sit-down dinners in our better restaurants in the States. And it is not all showmanship to take your mind off the taste of food. It tastes as good as it looks. That's quality!

Can we duplicate that degree of commitment to detail? The Marysville, Ohio, experience of Honda; Sony's experience in San Diego; Mazak in Florence, Ky.; and Nissan's in Smyrna, Tenn., prove there's nothing wrong with the American worker culturally that leadership, guidance, and the establishment of standards won't cure. (Perhaps food preparation and flower arrangement, which the Japanese have a particular knack for, are exceptions. Let's hope the proliferation of American fast-food franchises along the Ginza won't cause this unique Japanese talent to become extinct.)

There are, however, examples of American ability to attend to detail in food preparation. Consider Bruce and Kathy Gore, young Americans engaged in quality salmon harvest and preparation in Alaskan waters. In their operation, each fish is hand carried, hand rubbed, and hand glazed — perfect silvery specimens with not a broken scale and certainly none of the bruises that mar the average salmon. They are the Rolls Royces of frozen fish.

"When I first fished for salmon, we used pitchforks. Now I massage them; I am like a mortician, trying to make fish look better than they did in life," Bruce Gore told Phyllis C. Richman, *Washington Post* food critic and writer.[1] This is quality — and by an American couple who understands, as do the Japanese, that the customer is important and must be catered to and cultivated to keep his owner patronage.

Japanese Protectionism

"You cannot penetrate the Japanese market. Japan, Inc. is happy to export, but don't try to crack their domestic market. Their protectionist attitude creates a barbed wire fence around that country."

True or false? Either answer will net you partial credit. The Japanese quality standards are so high that you will see very few of the Big Three U.S. automakers' products on the road, other than official U.S. government vehicles. But the truth of the matter is that, for the most part, the quality of our U.S. products is inadequate to meet Japanese standards. Given the cost of our imports, the Japanese want to make sure they are *at least* comparable to the quality of domestically produced products.

"Yes, their quality is as good as advertised," says Bill Panttaga of Borg-Warner Kabushiki Kaisha. "They like our technology and know-how, but they don't like our inattention to detail. For example, one of our products will have a scratch on the casing and they'll reject it, even though the component otherwise is perfect. They just smile and say, 'if you're indifferent to how it looks on the outside, where we can visually inspect it, what will it be like on the inside?'"

Al Nakano, president of Kulicke and Soffa (Japan, Ltd.), a stateside company that produces electronic wire bonding machines, confirms the Japanese view of U.S. indifference to cosmetic appearances and operational defects. His company's machines cost twice as much as their Japanese counterparts, but they are superior and, after some redesign to meet Japanese desires, he has been able to move his product. His counsel to those who would seek Japanese market penetration: Try to understand cultural differences, offer a quality product, and exercise extreme patience.

Motorola and Westinghouse have likewise demonstrated that the Japanese market can be penetrated — *provided* American management is willing to put forth the effort.

THE KING OF THE HILL SYNDROME

Another *bête noir* of management is the feeling that we have a God-given right as Americans to be superior in all things. Are we really God's chosen people, second only to Israel?

It's hard to argue that we have not been blessed to an incredible extent by geography and resources. Neither Canada to our north nor Mexico to our south can claim equivalent advantages. Our form of government, capitalistic economy, climate, and free and open society are also unique blessings. But, to feel that these are givens — that we need do nothing to preserve our blessings — is wishful thinking of the grossest sort.

It is important to bear in mind that our natural resources were present when this country was peopled by its original inhabitants, the Indians. Without disparaging America's original inhabitants, it was the arrival of English and European settlers in search of religious and political freedom that developed this nation into an internationally recognized, compassionate, opportunity offering, and industrially and technologically advanced country. It was the blood, sweat, tears, and efforts of people with an indomitable will to be free and to succeed who accomplished, in a historically short period of time, the modern-day miracle, the United States of America, which stands as a shining example of the efforts and ingenuity of man, God's stellar creation. But, preservation and improvement of our assets will require ingenuity and effort.

QUALITY: THE BALL IN YOUR COURT

To be King of the Hill is no sin, as long as one recognizes the elements that made that achievement possible. Arrogance, incidentally, is not one of those elements, but arrogance is an attribute that has contributed significantly to the downfall of quality in America.

Art and literature offer examples that help make the point: An artist or writer who becomes famous after years of developing technique and talent often becomes lazy, self-centered, and arrogant because he can peddle anything on the strength of his name and reputation. He can peddle it until he finds himself swept off the hill by fresh talent that is willing to put forth the competitive effort to succeed.

U.S. industry has followed a similar course. Willing to work diligently and with purpose, industry has given this nation the highest standard of living and affluence in the world. World War II, with its ravages of the industrial production system in Europe and the Far East, left the United States undisputed King of the Industrial Hill. The three decades that followed created a "thus-it-is-and-thus-it-will-ever-be" self-ordination as far as industrial superiority was concerned. Management then turned its attention to exotic technology and high profits as the twin gods of production, without much thought to either the customer's desires or quality of the product.

Japan flung down the gauntlet and challenged our industrial superiority and our customer's loyalty. It is now essential that we accept the opportunity we have to reestablish ourselves as masters of the indomitable competitive spirit.

PEOPLE: THE ELEMENT OF SUCCESS

The final misconception is that people play no great role in attaining quality. In this age of high technology, computers, numerical control, computer numerical control, and flexible manufacturing systems, who needs people? Indeed, it is argued that, with the further development of robots and automation, the need for people (an unpredictable and often disagreeable barrier to management's success) may soon be removed. Won't automated factories of the future do away with the need for people? No.

Fanuc, Ltd., located near Mt. Fujiyama and Lake Yamonaka, has robots producing and testing robot components. The factory is large, poorly lighted, and unusually quiet. Robots don't need light to work, and they have no conversation other than the hum of their DC motors. Across the street, robots produce those DC motors. Automated carts make the rounds of each robot machining center to deliver motor components to production and assembly centers.

But, even in this highly roboticized plant, there are human workers. Why? The president and CEO, Dr. S. Inaba, explains: "Every six hours, machines must have chips removed from cutting and grinding tables. I've not yet been able to devise a machine that will accomplish that job on site."

Farther down the line, human workers put on bell housings. Why men instead of machines? Says Inaba, "The fit is most important, and I've not been able to design a machine with the visual-touch sensitivity that man can experience."

Regrettably, the development of automation and mass production lines have desensitized management to the difference between the sensibilities of man vs. the objectivity of machines. We find it easier, at times, to keep our inanimate machinery lubricated than to keep our subordinates "stroked." Unlubricated, the former will wear extensively and finally grind to a halt. The latter, unlubricated by recognition, reward, and understanding will continue to work, but at a slower rate; they'll become indifferent to what they're doing, and the result will manifest itself in poor product and service quality.

Machines can't communicate unhappiness with treatment accorded; nor can they influence the other machines. However, humans can. Unstroked, they become discontented and communicate this, which can have epidemic-like consequences.

Frequent layoffs and forced early retirements have contributed to the scope of U.S. quality problems. F. A. Schaeffer and C. E. Koop, in their interesting treatment of this question in *Whatever Happened to the Human Race?*, state, "Those who regard individuals as expendable raw materials — to be molded, exploited, then discarded — do battle on many fronts with those who see each person as unique and special, worthwhile and irreplaceable."[2]

People *are* important. At times they are the most unpredictable resource in one's network of responsibilities, but that should represent a challenge and a potential in the achievement of quality. People require your time and attention — but they are worth it. They create the computers and the programs; they write the symphonies and do the paintings that are timeless in their message and originality. No question about it — people *are* quality's most important resource.

Middle Management

While mobility in any organization is essential for motivation of junior comers, the rapidity with which U.S. management moves is ridiculous. Estimates in 1983 were that top managers normally hold their positions an average of three and one-half years. This means frequent direction and policy changes that break the continuity of purpose, planning, and ongoing programs. Trying to learn the new boss's idiosyncracies, interests, and management style while simultaneously keeping all the balls in the air can damage productivity. While it can be argued that frequent change brings in fresh ideas, the penalty often is that ideas of the previous regime are discounted before they have had time to mature. Additionally, the new top men may not be in the job long enough to be held accountable for any eggs they may lay.

Mobility in top management can also have a completely disquieting effect on long-range strategic planning. Anxious to see their own ideas play, short-term managers will be interested in establishing short-range productivity/revenue-producing goals that can be readily realized. This approach can be very hard on both personnel and the company over the long term.

One of the most critical responsibilities of management is long-range planning. It permits investment in capital improvements, research and development goals, work satisfaction enhancing programs, expansion plans — the rudiments of sound management. Next to an ignorance about the value of quality in the survival and growth cycle, management has been most delinquent in its long-range planning responsibilities.

Footnotes

1. Phyllis C. Richman, "Silver Harvest," *Washington Post*, 17 September 1985, sec. D1, p. 16.
2. Francis A. Schaeffer and C. Everett Koop, *Whatever Happened to the Human Race?* (Old Tappan, N.J.: Flemming H. Revell Co., 1979), p. 16.

CHAPTER 5

QUALITY IN EUROPE

Europe's reputation for quality lasted longer than its real ability to produce that quality because we "provincials in the colonies" revel in ownership of anything made in one of the big three — England, France, and Germany. At one time our assessment was based on our recognition of the fact that, prior to automation and production lines, our European forefathers were excellent craftsmen. If you wanted the best watch, you bought one with a Swiss movement. A photographer who could afford the best would buy a German-built Leica. The best china was France's famous Limoges or Haviland, and Irish Waterford crystal was the best crystal to be had. The world-class automobile was Rolls Royce, and the prestigious sports cars were Jaguar and Porsche. Note how many European leaders have been edged out by Oriental contenders.

IGNORING THE STATE OF THE ART

In 1982 in Frankfurt, I listened to Hans-Juran Meyer, vice president and senior department manager of the quality department of MAN's Mechanical and Structural Division, one of Germany's largest conglomerates producing a range of products from railroad trains to wind generators; I could close my eyes and imagine I was in the United States listening to a large defense manufacturer brief me on his plant's letter-perfect MIL-Q-9858A system. Meyer knows what is required to achieve quality.

"But does top management participate in MAN's quality program?" I asked during my visit in 1982. The *successful* engineer shook his head sadly and said, "I have little success in getting them involved."

This is another example of management being self-satisfied and ignoring the competition. In my several trips to Europe, I have never come upon any dearth of knowledge about what *needs* to be done, but there is a definite gap between that and what *is* being done.

PERCEIVED PROBLEM AREAS

Perhaps the greatest contributor to Europe's quality problem is ignorance. While Europe's industry suffered much the same destructive fate as Japan's during

WWII, the Europeans had a well-established quality reputation prior to that conflagration. They had merely to pick up where they left off after the war. Why didn't that happen?

At least two major perturbations occurred: one cultural, one technological.

Culturally, U.S. affluence and our post-war occupation of Europe impacted European culture in much the same manner that we impacted Japan and Korea. America's informality and lack of respect for age and position, a relaxed work ethic — all of these, while ignored by the older generation, were quickly accepted by European young people, producing a subculture that rebelled against established lines of discipline and authority.

Albert Schunck, foreign liaison director for I.G. Metalle, Germany's largest union, described the change that took place in Germany's work force. He mentions an increase in absenteeism and a growing indifference to the work ethic and dedication to perfection once commonplace in the Teutonic culture. And, he says, "With the exception of Volkswagen, industry has not really given robotics much thought." Herein lies the second impact — technology.

The 70s and 80s, building on the technology ushered in by both the Nuclear and Space Ages, have seen the introduction of electronic and mechanical complexity to industry, quantum in nature and scope. Tolerances are much less forgiving than before, requiring more diligence and know-how. I suggest that the decreased concern of the work force, coupled with the increased technological requirement, caused Europe's quality problem.

Documentation of the "Hidden Factory"

Europeans have yet to pay much attention to costs. This is perhaps the most important step European industry can take to avoid the hazards the United States has experienced and is still experiencing. Until one knows what and how much those hidden factory costs are, one cannot begin to solve the problems caused by nonconformance: poor quality, high scrap, and high rework.

I'll venture a studied "guesstimate" that Europe will meet its quality Waterloo in three to five years if European management doesn't awaken to a few of the facts of life regarding the essence of quality and how it is achieved. Hand wringing and exhortation won't solve the problem. Evaluation and action will.

INTERNATIONAL VENDOR FLAVOR

Europe is unique in that it's a community of sovereign nations, occupying a limited geographic area. This gives rise to marketing agreements that include co-production and multinational vendor coordination. This may be the most treacherous collection of tightropes any quality manager has to walk. Imagine yourself having to monitor and require quality of a vendor with whom you have a significant marketing potential. The danger of cross-cultural clashes demands diplomatic and politic negotiators.

International Market Orientation

In the United States, there is not a paucity of domestic market; in Europe, almost every industry has a foreign market just outside its very limited geographical borders. This may contribute to Europeans' apparent indifference to foreign competition. They have never known anything *but* foreign competition. However, the continental competition they have experienced is acceptably softened by a gentlemanly live-and-let-live understanding. The competition from the Far East plays hardball, and, while tariff barriers and quotas may stave them off initially, public demand will require that such artificial barriers eventually be lifted *or* competitive quality be achieved.

POSITIVE ASPECTS OF AND SUCCESSFUL COMPANIES IN EUROPEAN INDUSTRY

There are a number of European management approaches that might bear emulating. One involves relationships with unions. I.G. Metalle's Albert Schunck explains the co-determination relationship German unions enjoy with management: two levels of involvement exit, with one union level at the supervisory level and the second tier at the management level. Numerically, the supervisory-level union leaders equal plant-level members. At the management-director level, there are fewer members and they have, perhaps, less influence, but they exercise what Schunck terms a "co-determination" influence on issues such as "rules of the house," daily work hours, bonuses, holiday planning, and company social schemes. He points out that this is important since, under German law, the government can't intervene in strikes as the U.S. government can. Management's willingness to allow unions a voice in policy matters, even though not of parity status with management, apparently has contributed much to union/management harmony.

Unions are concerned about Japanese competition, but quality is not recognized as the issue. "Lower prices through higher production is the key," says Schunk. The inescapable relationship of quality and productivity is not yet appreciated, or so it would appear.

QUALITY: THE BALL IN YOUR COURT

Quality Circles

By and large, European industry considered quality circles a Japanese cultural phenomenon that had little value in Europe. The Citroen assembly plant in Rennes, France is an exception. At Citroen, assembly workers are enthusiastic about their quality circle, and they report that management is seriously interested in their input. The 11 circle members I interviewed claim their circle provides an active channel of communication with their bosses regarding production procedures, working conditions, and personnel problems. The circle members' responses demonstrate a great depth of understanding.

A. Genovese, plant manager, and L. Mercier, quality manager, obviously established quality circles on a solid foundation. According to Rene Le Gall, quality engineer for Citroen, the Rennes facility was Citroen's quality pacesetter.

Extensive Test Programs

Opel's assembly plant southwest of Frankfurt is an example of what extensive training does for quality. While rejecting quality circles, this plant achieves quality by subjecting its components, from seat fabrics to shock absorbers, to extreme life-cycle dynamic post-design testing. They do no source inspection, but they perform 100% receiving inspections. And, in 1982, Opel was beginning to look at robotics in the paint shop and in some areas of welding.

Another feature that makes the Opel a popular car in Europe is the integration of service into the producer's quality system. This provides comprehensive feedback for design and material corrective action.

Documentation

Telefonbau and Normalzeit, Germany's leader in communications and alarm systems, demonstrates an excellent data gathering and evaluation system. An automated system for data stowage permits them to retrieve data and determine trends. This ensures correction of problems before they become customer-related.

Apprentice Training

One of the strengths of German industry before and after the war is apprentice training. At Zettlemeyer, a subsidiary of IBH located in Konz, 8% of the workforce is in an apprentice program. It includes an exceptionally well-equipped classroom and shop area where apprentices spend half of their day under instruction and the remainder out on the production floor under the supervision of a journeyman craftsman. This three-year program ensures a continuity of talent and contributes significantly to Zettlemeyer quality.

Heinrich Von Prittwitz, managing director of sales and service for Zettlemeyer, explains that, while the firm is not into robotics yet, 60% of its machinery is numerically controlled or computer numerically controlled. Between '81 and '82, Zettlemeyer reduced scrap from 2.5% to 1.8% and was continuing on a down trend.

Quality Systems

SNECMA, one of France's larger producers of aircraft engines and landing gear, has a comprehensive quality system, but it has only moderate automation and no robotics. And, not surprisingly, there are no quality circles.

MATRA, a giant conglomerate with 11 major product lines ranging from missiles to automobiles, represents a company on the leading edge of technology. Its extremely sophisticated test and evaluation facility is impressive, but its lack of scrap and rework documentation and quality circles is not.

Unique Approach to "Defoding"

Dassault's plant at Argenteuil, a suburb of Paris, assembles the fuselage of the Mirage 2000 and F-1 jet fighters. There are two significant innovations in this plant. The first innovation: all new production models are first assembled by quality personnel. This gives them first-hand knowledge of problems production assemblies may expect, and, of even greater benefit, provides instant feedback to Dassault's major design/prototype facility in St. Cloud via a computer-aided design/manufacturing (CADM) system. This marriage of production, quality, and design ensures quality products on delivery.

Foreign object damage has been a significant cause of rework in U.S. overhaul and rework contractors' plants. Dassault's J.Y. Lazard explains that his firm solves the problem by rotating the jig-mounted fuselage around its horizontal axis. Everything not secure drops out. This second innovation is both practical and ingenious. Vive la France.

Renault — Coming Up Fast

Renault's plant in Flins produces 22% of Renault's worldwide output of 8,000 autos per day. Flins isn't Renault's most automated plant, but the fully automated corrosion control plant is impressive. It takes all guesswork and opportunity for human bobbles out of this important process. Welding is largely automated, and electrodes are replaced before they reach 50% of advertised life. This produces welds that are less than .03% defective. Unlike Toyota, where anyone is not only authorized but *encouraged* to stop the production line when a defect is detected, at Flins, no one short of the upper management level is authorized to stop the 1,800-car-per-day production line. "We just hope the customer doesn't find the defect," a spokesman said, who understandably did not wish to be identified. This reflects a tendency of too many U.S. industries where production is the key and quality is supported only to the extent it does not hinder production quota.

Quality in Composites

Since 1970, Dassault's composite fabrication and test facility in Biarritz on the southwestern coast of France has used composites for control, high-stress, and access panels on the Mirage III, F-1, Mirage 4000, 2000, Alfa jet, and Falcon 50, the latter of which is being purchased by the U.S. Coast Guard. Dassault began development of its composite capability in the Jaguar, but the first flight test of composite use in aircraft was in the Mirage II in 1975. Documentation of composite process control is comprehensive.

Dassault works closely with Surveillance Industrielle De L'Armement, the French Ministry of Defense counterpart to the quality section of the U.S. Defense Logistics Agency. Complete lamination is developed by the local design department of Dassault Biarritz, then approved by both SIAR and corporate quality before going into production. This assures a sound review process. All changes go the same route. Dassault is essentially establishing composite quality standards in France. In fact, some U.S. aircraft and space giants look to Dassault for ideas in this technological breakthrough.

Vendor control is achieved by specifying process control procedures, auditing compliance, and then double-checking by receiving inspection.

Environmental control is most critical. Temperatures must be kept between 20° C and 70° C, relative humidity between 40 and 70%. These same standards apply to stowage of the carbon, fibers, and resins. Since there are no French sources for fibers, these are imported from the United States, United Kingdom, and Japan.

Application and curing are delicate processes, and Dassault's evaluation of the effectiveness of the composite's bonding is most interesting. This is accomplished by both X-ray and ultrasonic inspection means. Results are printed out in color-coded graphics.

Dassault claims to produce less than 1% scrap. They don't offer specifics about rework.

Dassault's assembly plant in Merignac offers an example of the contribution a stout work ethic can make to quality. Assembly line organization and cleanliness reflect the pride in workmanship these aircraft assemblers have in the fruits of their labor.

PRESENT VERSUS FUTURE

By using examples of French and German industries that I visited, I've attempted to paint a word picture of quality in Europe. As a member of the NATO quality group that planned the 1984 symposium in Paris, I'm fairly well convinced that these two countries are representative of quality in the United Kingdom, Italy, and Belgium. From this, I believe a number of observations can be drawn.

First, why have some major European industries succeeded while the United States has taken severe, damaging hits? The relationship established between management and unions (the concept of co-determination), the recognition that layoffs damage continuity of skill and morale of craftsmen, that slowdowns are preferable, and that, as management goes, so goes the worker — all of these have combined to make industry more sensitive to the need for a team approach to manufacturing. Recent events indicate this may be catching on in the United States.

European automobile and aircraft industries tend to better identify poor design early on rather than delegating that function to the customer. As was implied by Alfred Schunck, Japanese industry still leads in this area.

The apprentice/journeyman's approach to a formal tiered training program ensures knowledgeable craftsmen.

Finally, the basic European work ethic contributes significantly to quality in Europe.

The four factors summarized — union-management relationships, more stringent test scenarios, apprentice training programs, and work ethic — comprise the basic underpinnings of quality in Europe.

BUT, ON THE OTHER HAND ...

While there are a number of positive areas in which European industry may take pride, there are warning signs that they may be approaching the same hazardous section of road on "Competition Parkway" that the United States has been navigating with great pain for the past several years. One of the warning signs is the lack of preoccupation by European management and customers alike regarding quality. This is a condition almost guaranteed to induce a quality crisis. While Japanese quality is recognized, there appears to be little concern over what this can mean to the European economy and industrial competitiveness.

QUALITY: THE BALL IN YOUR COURT

While European workers and consumers aren't yet as affluent as their U.S. counterparts, this is not far down the pike. This can have a serious impact on worker motivation and job satisfaction. Failure to appreciate the value of robotics and automation to the extent the Japanese have, will have a serious effect on Europe's competitive marketing of a quality product. While the very affluent can afford the exclusive hand tooling of a Rolls Royce, the average man on the street who would like to have a car comparable in styling and reliability cannot. He must rely on industry to bring cost down and reliability up. This can be most reasonably accomplished by automation and use of robotics.

The indifference to quality circles can also work to European industry's disservice. Europe's ethnic homogeneity gives its quality circles great promise and a solid potential for identifying and solving problems before they get out of hand.

Quality control, regrettably, is still based primarily on final inspection. As discussed previously, with low-volume and relatively simple products, this approach may be considered acceptable in some circles. However, when high volume and complex commodities are involved, process control is the only way to assure quality.

CHAPTER 6

SIXTY RUNGS IN JAPAN'S QUALITY LADDER

"He who wrestles with us strengthens our nerves and sharpens our skills. Our antagonist is our helper." Edmund Burke

If success is excuse enough for deification, we have transformed Japan into a place of worship, and the pilgrimages our business community makes to Japan are probably justified. Without question, in the past five years there have been many books and articles written on Japanese industrial success. Books by Japanese and American authors quickly reach best-seller status, confirming the fact that U.S. businessmen and customers alike are mesmerized by this rags-to-riches phenomenon in which the United States played a major role.

Is this an academic exercise Americans are going through, similar to our armchair reaction to television's "bad news from around the world"? Is this a self-flagellation to atone for the years we slept in self-satisfied stupor, confident no one could approach us industrially? Let's hope there's more to the widespread interest in our worthy competitors.

And let's do more than scratch the surface of the phenomena that transformed "Made in Japan" from a label signifying "cheap" to one signifying "quality, reliable, and preferable."

The Japanese quality phenomenon is not the product of quality circles, top management involvement, MITI protectionism, better education, or more disciplined workers alone. It is the product of 60 or more different factors, all of which impact on the issue of quality to a significant degree.

First of all, their success has been a direct result of market research and a focus on quality. During a visit to the Komatsu headquarters in 1982, Osamu Takahashi, managing director and general manager of Komatsu's R&D Division, described it. "In 1961, Caterpillar's capture of the Japanese tractor market made us realize we had to do something drastic to stay in business. We concluded that quality offered the biggest payoff. Our chairman announced a QC campaign in 1962. In 1963, we instituted quality circles, and in 1964, we won the coveted Deming Prize for quality. We built on the momentum that recognition gave us and, in 1981, we won Japan's highest honor for quality, the Japan Quality Control Award. We attribute these achievements to two things: research to determine the market needs and preference, and *quality* — fulfilling expectations the customer had specified or those we had created during marketing."

Kaoru Ishikawa, president of Musashi Institute of Technology, was equally frank during my initial visit to MIT. "After the years of deprivation caused by WWII, Japan began producing goods for the consumer market. Initially, we were sacrificing quality for production, and we earned a reputation of producing cheap junk. With the help of Deming and Juran, we began educating management to the need for quality. It was a top-down effort that eventually concentrated on foremen, since we felt they could communicate best with workers in the plants. This campaign included seminars, public radio broadcasts, quality control circles, and publication of *Gemba to QC* (a magazine, *QC for Foremen* in 1962). This monthly compilation of quality circle information was renamed *FQC* in 1973. It currently has a circulation of over 70,000 per month."

When queried as to whether he thought quality circles are viable in Western societies, Ishikawa replied, "Yes. Though the Buddhist mentality more easily lends itself to QC, I believe circles can profitably be used with some modifications in any culture." He cited Singapore, where three vastly differing cultures (Islamic-Malays; Buddhist-Chinese; Hindu-Indian/South Pacific) are mixed in an industrial society whose annual per capita productivity rivals that of Japan.

The following factors are not prioritized in any manner; they are simply 60 factors that, in my opinion, have contributed to Japan's dramatic post-war industrial recovery and its challenge to the world's other leading producer nations.

(1) *Lifetime employment.* By and large, Japanese workers retire at 55, but, once accepted for employment (especially in larger companies), they are *guaranteed* employment with that company. And, according to Masaharu Odaki, deputy general manager of Keihin works of Nippon Kokan Steel Co. (NKK), "Very few workers leave the firm after their second or third year." Tenure doesn't demotivate workers, Odaki says, "because workers recognize that their semi-annual bonuses depend on the economic vitality of the firm." At Komatsu, these total about 10 extra months of pay per year. In addition, perks include housing for unmarrieds, home loans for newlyweds, promise and fact of upward mobility within the company, access to an employe cafeteria, uniforms, and partially subsidized holiday trips.

Teruhisa Tanaka, manager of technological coordination (with NKK for 20 years), says he wouldn't consider leaving the firm even if he could get a substantially better position and salary. "Absolutely not. I will remain here till I retire," he says. "I am NKK and NKK is me."

Lifetime employment gives Japanese industry the advantage of a stable, experienced work force. The United States, on the other hand, is a mobile and ambition-driven society. Lifetime employment here is primarily practiced by very large industries. Where practiced, it is a definite factor in quality.

(2) *Company unions.* This approach to unionization lends itself to a better understanding between management and worker. Noriyuki Sugihara, ex-president of the company union at Yokogawa Hewlett-Packard (YHP), cites an example of the difference between Japanese and American unions. Asked whether he thinks his one-time constituents deserved a bigger piece of the profit pie, he replies, "No. My feeling is that quality improves productivity and, as productivity grows and we become more competitive, the "pie" grows. We don't look for a bigger piece of the pie — just a larger pie."

(3) *Bonus plans.* Most Japanese companies pay bonuses twice a year. These aren't bonuses in the strictest definition, but "saved pay" — an enforced saving that enables workers to make major purchases such as appliances or automobiles, to invest in "postal savings," or to make a down payment on a house. In essence, it is a fiscal year cushion to both company and employe. It can amount to almost a year's pay, as noted previously. It is a negotiated bonus in which union and management leaders participate (separate from pay negotiations).

The bonus system provides management flexibility to deal with market surges or recessions, since bonuses are conditional on meeting productivity targets. Should the market sour, should sales or profits fall, the company can reduce or withhold bonuses. Not a pleasant prospect, but workers prefer the loss of a bonus to being laid off during slow times.

Many workers invest their bonuses in Japan's famous "postal savings." These provide modest interest rates to the investor and serve as a source of expansion capital for industry. This keeps industry from having to depend on a reduced money market, with its high interest rates caused primarily by increased government borrowing.

(4) *Ethnic homogeneity of work force.* This has obvious advantages and a few equally obvious disadvantages. Japan tightly controls immigration and, thus, enjoys a cultural homogeneity of its work force. Management and labor share a language and cultural background, and goal regimentation of the Japanese work force is therefore much easier than in our heterogeneous society. Our many languages and cultural backgrounds — as well as our emphasis on freedom of thought and the individual — encourage questions, opposition, and disagreement. Our system has given birth to some of the greatest technological advances and has precluded ambitious rulers from leading us into national self-destruction by exploiting a national chauvinism, but a homogeneous society like Japan's is more adaptable to concepts like quality control circles and participatory management. While the Japanese think "we," Americans think "I."

(5) *Top management involvement in quality.* Japan's executives are personally involved with both the details and personnel of their business. They know their

personnel and can greet them by name because they get out on the floor, meet them, observe what they are doing, and are conversant about problems. They know the details of their companies' quality strategy since they are directly involved in its derivation and implementation.

Executives of all the Japanese firms I've ever visited wear the same uniforms as their workers, so it is difficult to identify them as top management. Their presentations, which key in on what they are doing to promote quality, quickly reinforce their understanding, and best of all, their involvement in quality. Perhaps the strongest cases made by management are made by Ken Sasaoka of YHP and Osamu Takahashi of Komatsu. Interestingly enough, the latter did not give nearly so much credit for turnaround to the United States as did Ishikawa of Musashi Institute of Technology. The total quality control system and top management QC audit are two examples of top management involvement.

(6) *Quality control circles*. Quality circles (by whatever label) are a way of life in Japanese industry. JUSE estimates that since the first circles were introduced in Japan (in 1960), the movement has grown to include more than a million circles with up to 14 million members. As mentioned before, the monthly *FQC* published by JUSE provides a vehicle to share quality and productivity suggestions and achievements throughout all industry. It appears to be widely read and is keyed to the worker/foreman level.

Since 1971, JUSE has sponsored competitions to recognize those circles that produce the most innovative and valuable quality improvement suggestions. Circles normally meet on company time, either weekly, bi-weekly, or monthly. At Nissan, in Oppamma, circles meet during lunch, breaks, or after work. That demonstrates the ultimate motivation.

Masumasa Imaizumi, of the quality and standards department at Nippon Kokan Steel, lists 10 characteristics of circles: self-development, voluntary participation, group activity, participation by all, application of QC techniques, activities relevant to the place of work, enlivening motivation for longevity's sake, mutual enlightenment, creativity and innovation, and consciousness of and thirst for quality improvement.

Sueo Ohnaka, manager of the special electronics engineering department of Fujitsu, says the firm has 2,600 quality circles. All suggestions generated by the circles are evaluated and the best are sent to top management. There are bonuses for the best ideas.

It is easy to see that circles not only solve problems but also broaden the worker's outlook, education, social intercourse, interpersonal relationships, growth and understanding that anything that profits their company profits them.

(7) *Use of robotics and automation*. Despite what American standards would represent as 4% unemployment, Japanese industry claims a shortage in skilled

labor. (They quote unemployment at 2%.) To augment the human work force, Japanese industrialists have embraced automation and robotics. The United States may hold a slight edge in the development of robots, but, in 1982, 59% of the world's robotics *applications* were found in Japanese industry. A prolific use is in the Oppama plant of Nissan, where robotic welding arms quickly and quietly slither through auto frame lightening holes to tack weld, retract, and head for another hole. These arms resemble eels playing hide and seek in a labyrinth. They have already claimed one worker's life when he disregarded their dedication to program.

Sadao Fujii, manager of Fujitsu's production technology development section, displayed robots being developed by Fujitsu. When queried about possible resentment by workers at being displaced by robots, he stated, "We concentrate on developing robots to do menial, repetitive, dirty, or dangerous jobs which workers do not like. Also, you must understand that we have a skilled labor shortage in Japan, and robots allow us to release workers to be retrained and take other positions." Fuji does admit that, at some time in the future, robots may compete with humans for more desirable jobs.

Robotics contribute significantly to productivity and quality. Cost of installation is quickly amortized by replacement of increasingly expensive human workers, the elimination of rework, the reduction of lighting and air conditioning requirements, and by reprogrammability. Most industries appear to be developing and programming their own robots, buying off-the-shelf components and designing systems to fill corporate needs.

(8) *Economic challenge*. Quality consciousness was Japan's basic answer to the economic challenge the country faced after WWII, when the reputation of Japanese consumer goods as "cheap junk" was associated with this manufacturing-oriented nation. Nippon Steel spoke of its inability to produce quality steel rapidly enough to be competitive. This led the firm to adopt automation.

An interesting sidelight was Nippon's claim that the environmental protection standards at their Kawasaki plant were stiffer than those found in the U.S. steel industry. (Twenty percent of NKK's $5 billion capital investment was spent to install pollution controls; 10% of annual operating costs keeps the system working.)

Nippon Steel has an oil-free operation; 93% of the energy is provided by coal/coke, the rest by gas. They say they have become the fifth largest world steel producer (second largest in Japan) because of modern facilities, people, and technology. They boast of 1,320 quality circles encompassing 8,500 workers, and scrap and rework are at a level of 7% compared to 27% in the U.S. steel industry.

(9) *Cultural proclivity for attention to detail*. Japanese gardens are living poetry, with neatly trimmed grass, flowers, and trees; Japanese restaurants have an equal concern for taste, appearance, and gracious service. The island is a "nation of inches" in the words of Ed Graham, in which every space, movement, and creation is optimized to ensure harmony with surroundings, usability, and appeal to greatest numbers. This attitude carries over into industry.

(10) *Superior education system.* Japan enjoys a 99% literacy rate — better than that of most nations that document such achievement. Primary and secondary schools work students hard and produce students who compete strenuously to gain admittance to prestigious colleges. Students have been known to commit suicide when they failed to gain acceptance to Tokyo University. The Japanese embassy points out that these students relax somewhat in college, but their commitment to secondary education lays the groundwork for a work force that understands effort as the key to success. Secondary education also prepares workers who, because of their literacy, understand work procedures and instructions better than Americans. Japanese schools concentrate on producing engineers (in 1981, 220,000 vs. 19,000 in the United States) rather than lawyers and accountants.

(11) *Commitment to training.* The Japanese don't believe workers can learn to produce quality by accumulating hands-on hours as do many American contractors. Formal training is a way of life, and Japanese industry provides resources to this vital area to ensure that workers know what they are doing. The concept that a lifetime employe is a part of the company's assets is reiterated time and again. As a company invests more and more in training, employes more and more become living assets, to be shifted to greater responsibilities, new positions, etc. Japan's low unemployment rate (in a work environment with the highest application of robotics) demonstrates that training and education are paying dividends.

Training commitment includes continual training of top executives in settings commensurate with position. JUSE conducts management training seminars at the nation's most plush resorts.

The next level of emphasis is the foreman — the interface between management and worker. The foreman's prestige is fortified by discrete training in quality, interpersonal communication, new processes, and trips abroad to observe other nations' productivity efforts. This appears to be accomplished much more easily in Japan than in the United States. The foremen are not the union men. Recall that employes elect company union representatives to convey their desires to management. One of the big advantages of such a company union is that the foremen are spared union stress — they're just as eligible as anyone else to be elected representatives, they participate in the election of their representative and, thence, can turn attention to the task at hand. Likewise, they can concentrate on training as appropriate, etc.

Fujitsu's Institute of Management Training is a classic example of Japanese industry's dedication to training. It includes a mandatory three-month course for executives who reach their 45th birthday. It serves to pump up and reignite this class to preclude any midlife slump.

(12) *National unity of effort.* Industry goals are coordinated by the Japanese Ministry of International Trade and Industry (MITI). Promising industrial ventures are backed by substantial low-interest, long-term loans provided by

banking consortiums. MITI plays the role of overseer in negotiating these loans. The short-term ROI is not their goal. Stockholders, though, do become impatient for return on investment, and considerable public relations work is required to convince investors that patience begets growth and profit.

Japanese trading companies (the counterpart of which our nation desperately needs in order to take advantage of developing nations that are rich in resources but dollar poor) play a vital role in arranging barter transactions and local co-production facilities taking advantage of less expensive human resources.

(13) *Foreman-centered QC training.* While Juran and Deming were responsible for "top-down" training and the concept of statistical QC, the Japanese themselves recognized that workers relate much better to foremen with whom they have constant close contact and to whom they are responsible than they do to top management. Therefore, why not provide first-level supervisors the training and resources to inculcate quality into the worker? They did this in 1962, and the effort has proved remarkably successful.

(14) *Financial incentive to the innovative.* While a pat on the back, a certificate, or an article in the plant paper might be adequate recompense for some, Japanese management recognizes the "yen talks." Those who make special efforts to improve quality and productivity — whether an individual or a quality circle — are financially rewarded. The twice-annual bonus is another incentive for increased effort and productivity.

(15) *Modern industrial base.* The Japanese have the United States to thank for this significant edge. After doing a relatively comprehensive job of destroying Japanese industry during WWII, our morality and generosity (plus our national security interest in making Japan self-sufficient) encouraged us to assist Japan financially and technically in rebuilding a modern industrial base. The Japanese are grateful for our help, but this does not deter them from trying to best us in the marketplace.

WWII left the United States untouched, so much of our industry is operating with equipment and facilities that predate the war. We are still recycling 1950 technology in our Industrial Plant Equipment program administered by the Defense Logistics Agency (DLA) . The equipment is stored by the DLA and made available to defense contractors, who pay only for the necessary refurbishment of equipment. It becomes "government-furnished equipment," saving contractors the expense of capital investment. Regrettably, it allows many defense contractors to ignore, for a time, the tough decision to modernize.

(16) *Quality recognition status.* A company that believes it has achieved the high standards of quality required by the 10 JUSE criteria may declare for the Deming Prize and invite the Deming Prize committee to evaluate its organization. The evaluators, professionals all, assess the achievements. The company must convince the committee that they excel in at least seven of the 10 categories. Very few achieve excellence of eight or more.

QUALITY: THE BALL IN YOUR COURT

The 10 criteria are:

1. Quality policy of the firm;

2. Organization and management;

3. Training and dissemination of quality policy;

4. Information collection, transmittal, and application;

5. Analysis — statistical quality control;

6. Standardization of quality control throughout organization;

7. Effectiveness (measure of effectiveness and conformance of pre-estimated result to actual result);

8. Quality assurance (safety and preclusion of product liability, process control, preventive maintenance, quality appraisal, and auditing system of assuring quality);

9. Effectiveness of quality control; and

10. Future plans to assure continuation of achieved level of product assurance.

The evaluated organization must score at least 70 points out of a possible 100 in the above categories to be awarded the Deming recognition. The highest grade the current executive director recalls was in the low 80s.

Five years after winning a Deming Prize, the firm is again examined to see if it has improved in its quality assurance. If such be the case, the organization is awarded the coveted Japan Quality Control Prize.

The Deming and Japan QC prizes are definite stimuli to quality consciousness in Japanese industry. Factories vie for such recognition, for it has sales value in the Japanese marketplace. Indicative of this is Sumitomo Metal's half-page ad in the August 24, 1981 *Wall Street Journal*, which included a large replica of the Deming Medal and the headline, "The Greatest Name in Japanese Quality Control is American." Though they won the award in 1953, Sumitomo still trades on that achievement.

Junji Noguchi, executive director of JUSE, points out that, through 1985 — the 35th anniversary of the Deming Prize — 48 individuals have been awarded the coveted Deming medalist award and 107 companies and nine factories have been honored the application prize. Thus, an average of three companies and 1.3 individuals per year have been recognized. High, uncompromising standards have kept the winners circle small but the prestige high.

A similar recognition, perhaps monitored by the American Society for Quality Control or the American Productivity Center, could achieve similar management recognition of quality in this country, with an industry payback in marketing similar to the Japanese experience.

(17) *Union of Japanese Scientists and Engineers (JUSE)*. This very active organization was established in Japan in 1946 with the specific charter to improve quality. Totally private, it now boasts a membership of over 1,850 companies, plants, and industries. Membership is limited to top management (not primarily of professionals, as is the American Society for Quality Control).

JUSE's thrust is *training*. As mentioned previously, it publishes the periodical *FQC* and numerous other pieces of literature on quality. It sponsors the Deming and Japanese quality competitions, the Ishikawa Award (for individuals making a literary contribution to quality), and an annual quality circle competition. JUSE is a most aggressive and potent factor in Japanese quality. There is no connection between JUSE and the Japanese government. Unfortunately, there is presently no U.S. organization with the same ability to broker international attitude, image, and performance of members.

(18) *Lack of government intrusion into quality*. What kind of resourcing and control can one get from the Japanese government? None. And that's the way Japan's private sector wants it. Comments one hears: "Too much red tape." "Interference and delay." Japan Productivity Center Director Mikio Aoki says, "We find no advantage from government intervention in quality with the possible exception of the coordinating support from MITI in promoting international trade." (Few American politicians or businessmen will agree that that's government's sole role.)

Japan's military production is minuscule by comparison to consumer goods. The Ministry of Defense does monitor the quality performance of defense-related commodities in much the same way our Defense Contract Administration Service does, but Japan's defense budget is so small that the consequence of this monitoring is insignificant. (It is interesting to note that MIL-Q-9858A is the model for conformance standards.)

(19) *Administrative reform of government regulations*. Japan's Prime Minister's Ad Hoc Committee on Regulation Reform focuses on deleting or modifying those regulations deemed liable to hamper industrial growth and quality. All in industry agree that the committee performs a positive function. Committee membership includes nongovernment agencies, such as JUSE and the Japan Productivity Center, as volunteer participants, and these overseers ensure minimum government intrusion into the affairs of commerce.

(20) *Meticulous analysis of productivity factors and trends*. The Japan Productivity Center was established in 1955, inspired by the Anglo-American Council on Productivity (the model for the European Marshall Recovery Plan). The center was the brainchild of Kohe Goshi, who had traveled to Europe and had observed the utility of the Anglo-American Productivity Conference and European Productivity Agency. Japan Productivity Center Executive Director Aoki points out that, "In Japan, personnel expenditures are considered a 'fixed cost,' much the same as facilities are considered."

QUALITY: THE BALL IN YOUR COURT

Aoki feels that we in America expect too little from workers who, therefore, never realize their full potential. His productivity charts show that, while overall economic productivity in the United States is higher than in Japan, our trend is nearly flat, while Japan still shows a steep upturn. He is certain this indicates that Japan will soon surpass U.S. productivity.

(21) *Consensus management.* Japanese managers, unlike their U.S. counterparts, do not make unilateral decisions affecting production, improvements, or quality. An idea or concept is aired for workers and middle management to comment on, and these observations and suggestions are all seriously considered by top management. This, of course, prolongs the Japanese decision-making process, but it distributes ownership to the corporate body through consent. (It also allows *all* to share blame for bad decisions.)

Because top management subscribes to quality control, and because responsibility for decisions is widely distributed, quality is not the compartmentalized concern it sometimes is in U.S. firms. Does this consensus approach preclude top management having the final say? Not at all. What it does is dispel the feeling of arbitrary autonomy.

The Japanese are not comfortable with the top man making all the decisions, and the top man is also somewhat uncomfortable in that role. The principal reason for this is not generally understood by Americans. It is that, if many participants are allowed to comment on an idea or policy change *before* it is locked in concrete, there will be much less resistance to it when implemented. All will identify with the policy and have a feeling of ownership. In addition, consensus affords an immediate review at the action level, which ofttimes prevents management from issuing an infeasible mandate. In America, too often we issue the mandate and then spend the next two years trying to have it accepted.

(22) *Work ethic.* Despite American influence on the Japanese consumers' tastes in clothes, music, and food (I saw more McDonalds, Wendys, and Pizza Huts on the Ginza than might be thought possible), Japanese workers have the same work ethic that the United States had before our workers came to feel they owe little to their companies. The Japanese have been accused of being a "nation of workaholics." The statement is meant as an insult, but they regard it as a compliment.

(23) *Resource limitation.* Japan, with its limited space and paucity of resources, must make the most of all they have. Japan entered WWII seeking territorial and raw material gains, and when their military solution failed, they turned to maximizing what they had. Space is at such a premium that it must be exploited with great care and diligence. This colors the Japanese workers' efforts to excel with what little they have — an example of adversity's positive influence.

(24) *Early retirement.* Do Japanese workers enjoy a predictable monthly income from their firms after retirement? In the majority of cases, no. They receive a lump-sum payoff that, together with meager social security benefits, must support

them for the rest of their lives after 55. As a consequence, they save and invest their bonuses and establish post-retirement "mom-and-pop" businesses, or become vendors as described in rung 26. There is an incredible number of small shops and groceries competing for the market.

Supermarkets, for the most part, have not caught on in Japan as they have in the United States. Early retirement (average age 53) keeps the labor market dynamic and does not appear to have been deleterious to individual longevity. Japanese men have the longest life expectance of any culture — an average life span of 89 years. Of interest is the fact that Nihon Kokan Steel has upped the retirement age of its worker to 60 in order to help employes and the company. Other industries may follow suit.

(25) *Uninhibited transition from government service to private industry.* Unhampered by the military/industrial complex phobia of the United States, top leaders in industry and commerce frequently are government or military retirees. Instead of starting in business and moving to government after success, the Japanese government bureaucrat, having learned the government organization well, moves to industry and uses his knowledge and contact to promote the economy. It appears to work better than our reverse system.

(26) *Hub/spoke development of vendors.* Japanese industry enjoys high vendor quality because many vendors are former employes who, having learned the parent companies' systems of quality, set up small "bike shops." Understanding quality manufacturing, they can provide quality components with little source inspection and few rejects. Many industries help finance such starts with venture capital. Toyota, for example, has "grown" 90% of its own suppliers (according to embassy estimates) with such venture capital. Competition is keen and nonconforming producers die, but the surviving organizations are indeed producers.

(27) *Application of Juran and Deming principles of quality control.* The Japanese are good listeners, and they are superb adapters of technology. They have no reluctance to exploit others' developments, and they identify with their philosophical and technical quality godfathers: J.M. Juran and W. Edwards Deming. While U.S. and European industry gave scant heed to these quality giants, Japan treated them with respect approaching traditional ancestral worship. The logo of the Deming Prize on a product, such as a Pentel pen, carries as much weight as appointment by Her Majesty, Queen Elizabeth II, does for Chandler and other companies in England.

(28) *Market research.* Komatsu points out that its rise to eminence in the heavy construction equipment field was the product of two thrusts — quality and market research — determining what consumers want and giving it to them.

U.S. manufacturers failed to perceive that the 1972 fuel crisis would have a real impact on the American buyer and continued to produce large, fuel-inefficient cars. The Japanese, already in the small car ascendency, saw a need and filled it. It is interesting to note that a few years ago GM conceded this market to the Japanese, stating that they could not produce this type of car as economically as could Japan. Now, with investment in Saturn, they have thrown down the gauntlet and declared themselves a competitor for the market.

(29) *Long-term management outlook*. U.S. top management turns over every three to three and one-half years and thus looks for short-term gains. The Japanese feel that the future is long term. Their investments (hard and soft) aim for growth over the long period. It's not hard to make a tortoise-and-hare analogy. Lower interest rates also help in this regard.

(30) *Industry commitment to research*. The Japanese government funds only 22% of the private sector's R&D — only half the U.S. government's investment. This permits a more market-oriented investment of R&D resources, which certainly benefits industry.

(31) *Competitive spirit*. Japanese industry functions in a more consumer-oriented environment than does U.S. industry. Japan's small defense budget effectively subtracts military contracts from industries' priority considerations, and competition for consumers' approval increases. In an intensely competitive environment, one has to try harder to win market shares. This stimulates quality, since quality wins customers, as car sales prove.

(32) *Self-mation*. This unique development of the Japanese auto industry allows manufacturers to prevent an automated line from getting out of adjustment and putting out a series of unsatisfactory parts. "Self-mation" involves a sensor which, when a machine begins making parts that are out of tolerance or defective, halts the machine and calls attention to the error.

(33) *Candor and consensus management*. Perhaps one of the most revealing observations in my interviews with Japanese industry is the candor they display in giving credit where credit is due (e.g., quality assurance lessons from Deming, Juran, and Feigenbaum). They are equally candid in admitting that theirs is, by and large, a management by consensus — total involvement of management in making decisions affecting product or production. Workers participate through quality circles.

(34) *Just-in-time inventory*. Japanese dedication to quality has brought them the additional advantage of low inventories, which reduce capital investments in materials, storage space, material handling equipment, and labor. Toyota boasts of a two-hour inventory. The Sony factory in Ichinomiya claims that vendors' trucks roll in every 90 minutes to keep up with a production rate of one Trinitron color TV or VCR every six seconds. This requires an excellent understanding between Sony and its vendors.

(35) *Vendor quality*. Just-in-time inventory is impossible without an assurance that vendors can produce quality goods. The every-90-minute appearance of vendors' trucks is meaningless if the trucks are forced to do double duty hauling defective

merchandise back to the vendors. No manufacturer can maintain a two-hour inventory if the next supply run may contain 10% unusable materials.

Failure to maintain the buyer's standard of quality generally means failure of the vendor's business — certainly it ends the vendor's relationship with the buyer.

(36) *Quality standards.* Zero defects is the unwritten but well-understood quality standard of Japanese industry. At a Sony factory, one can see a color TV which has been operating eight hours a day since December 1970 (37,000 + operating hours with no adjustments or repairs) still producing an acceptable picture. The industry standard is 10,000 hours.

(37) *Trading companies.* Quality is also stimulated by new markets, and Japanese trading companies provide this stimulus to industry. In a constant search for resources, the trading companies pave the way to barter manufactured goods for needed resources. Hard currency comes from countries such as the United States. This system gives Japanese industry the best of all worlds — new business in yen-poor markets and needed resources and dollar markets where quality is important. Sears, Roebuck & Co. began such a trading company in America; regrettably, it did not survive.

(38) *Line-stop authority.* In Toyota plants, every worker station has a line-stop button or switch. Each worker is authorized to stop the production line if something goes awry. The worker does not fear reprisal for interrupting production. The point is patently clear: quality transcends production schedule.

(39) *Venture capital from savings.* The Japanese save more than four times as much as we Americans do — about 20% of their personal incomes. An average working family of four has the equivalent of a year's wages in savings. When bonus times roll around, about 35% of that amount is put into savings for a rainy-day need or that big yen purchase which exceeds normal cash flow availability. As a result of this thriftiness, there is adequate venture capital in Japanese banks (at low rates of 7%) for modernization, expansion, and new starts. The first two contribute substantially to quality.

(40) *Face-saving and peer pressure.* Identification with firm and product makes each worker his own best quality standard. At Nissan, for instance, the quality people are at the end of the line in final acceptance. Production workers perform in-process checks. They are responsible for ensuring their own operations are done properly, but they also check the operation just previous to their stations. It is easy to see the peer pressure of having a production line colleague call attention to an inadequately performed operation.

(41) *Constant improvement.* As Deming is quick to point out, the only acceptable quality standard is one of constant improvement of process and product. The Japanese are avid practitioners of this philosophy.

QUALITY: THE BALL IN YOUR COURT

At Nitsuko, a modest-sized manufacturer and assembler of telephone equipment, a sign — in both Japanese and English — prominently displayed in the production area advises, "The first requirement of the job is to have an inquiring mind." Thinking is not only allowed, it's encouraged. T. Fuji, the managing director, says, "We are not selling telephone equipment. We are selling quality." This is the essence of competitiveness.

(42) *Customer satisfaction*. The customer, a flesh-and-blood human with tastes and distastes — not a faceless, formless impersonal market — is another important aspect of Japanese success. They understand fully the Golden Rule of business: "He who has the gold, rules." The customer, whether he be a prime contractor, the man on the production line, or the ultimate man-on-the-street consumer, is of consistent concern to the Japanese. What are his tastes? How can we innovate to pique his curiosity about our product? How can we assure that our product is going to give trouble-free service far beyond the warranty period? How can we be responsive to the customer when a breakdown occurs? From design and production to packaging, the Japanese pay attention to detail for the customer's benefit.

(43) *Plant exists for employes' benefit*. In a 1984 U.S. survey, 500 executives were asked their most important responsibilities. Customer satisfaction appeared fifth. Workers' welfare was seventh. By comparison, at Tokyo Juki, a manufacturer of commercial sewing machines, office equipment, computers, tailoring, and commercial cleaning equipment, President Takeo Yamaoka states, "Our business exists for the workers — to provide them jobs and fulfillment in life." This is not to imply that customers are unimportant to Yamaoka. On the contrary, he understands that quality products that give competitive market advantage can be produced only by employes who feel they are more than clock numbers.

(44) *Directors chosen from within company*. Japanese directors are normally chosen from inside the organization. In U.S. companies, most directors originate from outside the corporate structure. While this may inject a degree of objectivity and fresh innovation into the boardroom, it is unlikely to provide a detailed understanding and experience of the business at the decision-making level.

(45) *Nommunication*. Here's an example of the synergism that results when workers identify with one another and their company. "Nommunication," Noguchi of JUSE explains, "is what takes place when Japanese workers and management meet at the local bar or restaurant to relax, have a few beers or sake, and discuss their business. It creates a sort of after-hours quality circle where problems, solutions, and new ideas are discussed."

(46) *Job rotation*. U.S. unions have doggedly insisted on members working only within their narrow disciplines. In Japan, workers are rotated to different jobs with their unions' blessings. This gives management wide latitude in dealing with peaks and valleys caused by a changing market. This approach to job assignments is being effectively used in the United States by Nissan in Smyrna, Tenn. Workers

there increase their earnings in proportion to their ability to do different jobs. When unexpected resignations, death, retirement, or sickness occur, there is no question of having in-house talent to continue production without a hiccup.

(47) *Suggestion program.* In America, some suggestion boxes attract industrious spiders to build cobwebs and collect dust. In Japan, suggestion systems stimulate a harvest of ideas generated by workers — those most capable of seeing flaws in their manufacturing systems. Fuji Electric boasts of one employe who submitted 5,000 suggestions in one year. This is unusual, no question, but is indicative of the enthusiasm and value of the Japanese approach to utilizing in-house brain power. Recognition, reward (though it is token at times), and prompt processing and feedback are the keys to the success of their programs. Eight- to 14-month delays in feedback, petty jealousies and envy on the part of the reviewing team, and penurious payoffs are all symptoms of the illness in the U.S. system.

(48) *Favorable environment.* Does a person's work environment make any difference in his productivity? Without question. It affects the attitude he maintains about his job, his productivity, and the quality of his work. Cleanliness, orderliness of stowage and production flow, lighting and sound levels, and company uniforms, jackets, and caps, all make the employe feel valued. In plants where a combination of poor lighting, lack of floor space, lack of cleanliness, and disorderliness make the place look like a jungle, workers are demotivated and unproductive.

(49) *Utilization of managerial engineering techniques.* Can management use the same disciplined techniques of engineers? Yes. Ryuji Fukuda, currently one of Japan's most sought-after consultants in the United States and Europe, has written a book which should be a must on the senior manager's reading list. Titled *Managerial Engineering* and published by Productivity, Inc., it approaches management as a discipline that can be structured and performed in much the same manner that engineers approach problem solving or technological advances. The reactive mode of management is not competitive. To regain leadership, we must be proactive, use all our resources, anticipate problems, and prevent their occurrence. Is it possible to achieve this? It's possible and necessary. Reaction isn't management.

(50) *Company loyalty.* Many mistakenly believe that company loyalty is achieved by the much-publicized Japanese company exercises, motto repetition, or singing. It goes much deeper and broader. It consists of a working relationship that causes workers to recognize that the company is truly concerned, not only about the customer and the product, but about them.

Bonuses, lifetime employment, working conditions, quality circles, suggestion programs, equipment, training, recognition — all of these build employe loyalty. They allow a worker to say, "I am worth something to my employer. I am not just a clock number to be laid off when the economy is in a downturn. I am a valued employe whose opinions are not only sought, but whose suggestions, whether they be individually generated or corporately derived in a quality circle, are important to the welfare and competitive success of this company. This company is me, and I am the difference I make in whatever I do. I can never be guilty of giving my company less than my best efforts."

(51) **Banks vs. individuals as stockholders or financiers.** Money to begin, to expand, to grow is an important factor of quality. Unfortunately, U.S. management often believes stockholders are after short-term gains instead of what the investor actually would prefer. In Japan, most large companies are financed by banks and other financial institutions, and these institutions recognize that a well-founded, visionary business ensures not only return and long-term gains, but the opportunity for an investment bonanza. If U.S. businesses would assure investors that they are in the market for the long run, those investors might not feel inclined to seek short-term gains.

(52) **Cost consciousness.** What's our production cost and how does it compare with our competitor's cost? The Japanese are big spenders in their marketing efforts, but they do watch the cost of doing business, recognizing that this has a great impact on profitability. Being as resource-poor as they are, they are also sensitive to waste in their raw materials and administrative expenses.

(53) **Successful management of change.** U.S. businesses have difficulty managing change. Mergers, market perturbations, takeovers, economic downturns, strikes, product change, customer dissatisfaction, natural disasters, and the like upset the norm. We enjoy the comfort routines afford.

When change is the result of careful planning, it will normally result in acceptance and success. A Japanese market entrance is generally the result of studied research, careful evaluation, and resource support that is willing to take a loss until the venture can get a strong grip on the market. Too often, U.S. firms wait until buggies are obsolete before stopping buggy whip production. We fail to read signs that indicate a changing market and react. MITI helps Japanese industry keep an eye open for opportunities and supports industries that have the leadership and motivation to pursue such initiatives.

(54) **Personnel selection based on potential.** Few question that people are the single most important element in quality; yet, U.S. hiring practices are superficial and shallow. Tokyo Juki President Takeo Yamaoka says, "Selection of personnel is the most important phase of quality. We screen people very carefully and base our selection on two principle criteria: First, does the person really want to work for Tokyo Juki? Second, what is the applicant's potential? We are interested in what an applicant has achieved, but we feel his or her potential is much more important. How can an employe grow with us? What can he or she contribute?"

This philosophy is echoed by Marvin Runyon, president of Nissan America: "We are interested only in people who want to identify on a long-term basis with Nissan America. After a very careful screening and training period, the prospective employe interviews with the foreman he or she will work for. Then, if the new hire doesn't work out, human resources can't be blamed."

(55) *Contribution to society*. The Japanese feel an obligation to their society. They credit it with enabling them to succeed. In the United States, we often take our society, as well as our people, very much for granted. Japanese managers believe that business exists to contribute to society, not to exploit it.

The seriousness of this obligation was demonstrated in the early '80s by a Japanese skipper who committed suicide because his ship got caught in a storm that did much damage to his cargo of new cars. He felt he had failed to live up to his responsibility. Even more recently, when a Japanese 747 lost a vertical stabilizer causing it to crash with a loss of 520 lives, the chairman of the airline resigned. On our side of the pond, companies dump toxic waste indiscriminately, violate safety procedures, and release poisonous gasses with little concern except to wonder how their firms will survive.

(56) *Timing (or just plain luck)*. Taiichi Ohno, originator of Toyota's just-in-time inventory system, says the biggest contributor to Toyota's success is: "Luck and timing. When the gas crisis came, we had a product ready to take advantage of the market. It was a matter of timing!"

Of course, timing had little to do with Japan's success in the electronic watch, optics, or camera fields — that was pure quality.

(57) *Market demand*. Fuji film has been on the market for many years now, but it was not until the 1984 Olympics that it was readily available everywhere. Fuji had targeted that event for its serious market entry, and the firm heavily advertised Fuji as the official film of the 1984 Olympics. It had determined that Kodak — long the predominant film in the market — was vulnerable to challenge, and, groundwork done, Fuji made its move.

(58) *Investment of profits*. Plowing profits into a business to enhance its competitiveness makes good sense. Too often, however, the temptation to acquire new businesses — about which we know little, but which appear to diversify us — overwhelm us. At a time when competitive advantage did not depend on a discriminating customer, diversification might have been a proper decision. However, the time now dictates that we provide whatever resources are necessary to make changes and improve performance and product that will win the customer's loyalty. The Japanese operate on this premise; Komatsu is a case in point. When faced with severe competition from Caterpillar, they focused on and invested in quality, and now Komatsu sales centers are a common sight here on Caterpillar's home turf in the United States.

(59) *Published policy*. Policy is the published heartbeat of any organization. This written document tells management and workers what the business is and what is expected of employes; it also establishes the customer's preeminent status. It is signed by the CEO and promulgated in such a manner that all hands understand its contents and application to them. It is not an optional directive. It is *the word*.

QUALITY: THE BALL IN YOUR COURT

Too often U.S. companies fail to publish a quality policy, expecting people to intuitionally understand what is desired. This can be a fatal omission.

Japanese management establishes standards of expected behavior, productivity, and quality. Then they audit the results closely enough to ensure accountability of the individual.

(60) *Importance of the individual.* The importance of people has been alluded to a number of times in this chapter. If there is one preeminent rung in the Japanese success ladder, it has to be their true concern for people. Japanese concern isn't superficial or supercilious. It's not like the indifference that led to the formation and growth of U.S. unions. The mere image of concern never nurtures identification with or loyalty toward the corporation. It produces clock-and-boss watchers whose definition of "good enough" is "anything I can get away with." It produces subordinates who never "tell it like it is." They say what the boss will accept. Are people important to the Japanese executive? In successful companies, they are, without exception.

How many rungs are transferable? As least 50 of the 60 can be adapted by U.S. industry — some more easily than others — but in time, all contributing to our enhanced quality. The five out of reach are:

4. *Ethnic homogeneity of work force* — For obvious reasons;

8. *Economic challenge* — Blessed with land and natural resources, the United States has many decades before resource scarcity will be a problem;

9. *Cultural proclivity for attention to detail* — Japan's limited space and resources encourage attention to detail; American surplus discourages it;

23. *Resource limitation* — Cannot be a motivator for the foreseeable future; and

33. *Consensus management* — When we elect or appoint a president or chairman of the board, we expect that person to make decisions and want to hold them accountable.

What is Required?

The question remains, what is required to adapt Japan's positive forces to American industry and our population's psyche? The answer lies in *leadership* — leadership, in both government and industry, that sets goals, motivates, and leads the way by example.

Visits to Japan to witness the effect of leadership on quality and productivity are justified, but only to the degree that the sojourn excites the sensitivities and understanding of *why* the Japanese have achieved worldwide recognition for their successes in the marketplace and quality.

CHAPTER 7

KOREA –
THE AWAKENING GIANT

Tokyo's international airport at Narita now resembles America's corporate convention center, but within the next five years the scene will shift to Kimpo in Seoul, Korea. Many of the ingredients that contributed to our own industrial downfall appear to be present in Japan's economy: a growing budget deficit which will inevitably require an increase in taxes (a value-added tax is a leading contender), inflation, and affluence — all are factors which may well put a damper on Japan's industrial ardor.

Korea, on the other hand has a labor pay scale that will permit it to compete for markets in any area for many years to come. Also, Korean workers seem indefatigable, logging six- and seven-day work weeks and 10- to 12-hour work days. Vacations? "No vacation," said one Korean executive. "Plenty of time off for Christmas, funerals, Liberation Day, and Buddha's birthday." This work ethic is a key building block in any market takeover.

THE "LUXURY" OF REWORK

The Daewoo Shipbuilding and Heavy Machinery (DSHM) shipyard in Okpo is most impressive. The dry dock measures 530 x 131 x 14.5 meters and can accommodate a 1 million dead-weight ton (DWT) vessel. It can be separated into three sections to permit customization of the dock to fit various needs. A 900-ton traveling Goliath crane (aptly named) spans the 131-meter width of the dock. As a sample of Daewoo's capacity, on a typical day, the dock's three sections might be loaded with seven semisubmersible drilling rigs (each 260 x 200 x 116 feet), a 140,000 DWT bulk carrier, two 17,500 DWT product carriers, a barge-mounted seawater treatment plant, and a back-up drilling rig.

This dock has all the facilities and equipment for a world-class shipbuilding and heavy machinery fabrication source. The facilities are (as of 1983) woefully under-utilized (no doubt occasioned by the worldwide cutback in shipbuilding), but no expense has been spared in making Daewoo one of the most competitive shipyards in the world, with total quality control (TQC) and quality circles playing a significant role. The 170 organized circles generate their own agendas, and final evaluation of ideas that cross departmental lines are made at the headquarters level.

71

A strong quality policy prefaces the rather substantial quality manual. It includes the following: "The systems and procedures contained in our QA program are mandatory, . . . deviations will not be tolerated."

Unfortunately, there is no apparent system for collecting nonconformance data, without which there is no way to ensure process control. One must discover where errors and deviations are being generated. Daewoo's answer is, "We *do it over* as often as necessary to satisfy the customer." Daewoo can afford that attitude only as long as the $3 per hour labor rate holds. If worker expectations grow, a true systems approach to quality control will become mandatory.

Daewoo has another potential weak spot in its quality program: the quality organization is fragmented, and there's a quality system at only one of Daewoo's major yard divisions. (This weakness is also present in some large U.S. corporate entities.)

SHOE QUALITY

Kukji Corporation in Pusan turns out 200,000 pairs of shoes a day. These range from Nike tennis shoes and joggers to boots and overshoes. Their work week consists of six 10 and one-half hour workdays that include an hour for lunch and two one-half hour coffee breaks to relieve the tension of production line work. While there is little automation in this very labor-intensive plant, quality is excellent. There is less than 0.01% scrap, and that is burned for fuel. Rejects and returns from customers amount to 0.5%. These low scrap and reject rates are attributable to two factors: the high quality standards established by Kukji for their workers, and tough statistical sampling of shoes during production. New product lines are also tested rigorously.

Kukji and Education

About 3,000 of Kukji's 18,000-person work force are teenage females who for their 10 and one-half hour days receive $100 a month, room and board, and an opportunity to go to school after work. The latter is considered a real dividend for these girls who would not otherwise have this educational experience. Regular production workers receive from $150 to $250 a month for their efforts. At the high end, this represents less than $1.50 an hour. There is also a bonus system that includes a month's pay at the lunar New Year and a similar bonus on National Thanksgiving Day.

POSCO

The Pohang Iron and Steel Co. (POSCO), located in Pohang, is so clean and orderly, it's difficult to believe it is the world's sixth largest operating steel mill. This 2,200-acre mill has its own port, three steel and four blast furnaces, and a production force of 14,500. It produces 9,100 long tons of steel/iron per year. This figure was achieved only 10 years after the mill's initial production year, 1968, when 2,100 long tons were produced.

Even though 96% of its ore and 100% of its coal are imported, this $3.6 billion complex produces the most inexpensive steel in the free world — $422 per long ton compared to $560-600 for Japanese steel and $800 for American steel. Half of POSCO's capital investment has been repaid, and by 1988, the debt will be zero. Such rapid loan repayment is achievable only by producing a competitive product. The fringe benefit is the loan-eligible image it projects. Capital investment by banks, not stockholders, is an advantage.

Quality's Role

Quality performance at POSCO is meticulously recorded, as is analysis of results. For example, in 1973, it took 550 kilograms of coke to produce a long ton of steel. That figure has since been cut to 477-480 kilograms. In 1973, 50 kilograms of oil injection were required; by 1983, POSCO was an oil-less operation.

Some 1,900 quality circles operate to identify manufacturing quality/productivity problems and correct them. This is on the administrative, sales, and production side. Top management sets goals and work standards and monitors their implementation and support.

Worker Job Satisfaction

Since Pohang is somewhat remote from Seoul, POSCO has invested in 2,600 housing units to accommodate 4,346 families and bachelor dorms for another 4,031 workers. Included are schools to ensure workers' children ample preparation for the extremely difficult college boards. Houses are purchased through interest-free loans provided by POSCO. There are no unions, since workers' committees negotiate any requirements or misunderstandings with management. These management-labor councils meet monthly.

Bonuses of one month's salary are paid quarterly to POSCO's labor force. If business is above average, bonuses are increased to total six months of wages.

Madison Avenue Brief

The Japanese are not the only people from the Western rim of the Pacific basin who visit abroad and take notes. POSCO provides visitors an introductory briefing that includes slides and a Harvard-accented narrative that would do any major U.S. corporation proud. POSCO Executive Vice President Intaek Kim's rapid recitation of company statistics identifies him as a man who is involved in details. Expansion plans include a new plant in Gwangyang, on the southern tip of Korea. Construction began in July '85, with a projected March '88 completion. This will add 2,700 long tons of production capacity.

SAMSUNG GROUP

The literal translation of Samsung is "three stars." Samsung Electronic Company's symbol is a tri-star that stands for quality, technology, and good service. What better epitomizes a customer's desires? This obviously accounts for the Samsung Group's financial growth from 3.0% of Korea's GNP in 1974 to 7.9% in 1981. Samsung, in the Kyungri-Do area of Seoul, is now among the top 30 electronic products plants in the world. Products range from linear integrated circuit boards to refrigerators. In product range and production capability, Samsung Electronics is impressive, and the firm's originality of technology applications disputes the concept that Japan and Korea have nothing original.

Worker Quality Audit

All 15,000 Samsung personnel, regardless of assignment, receive formal training before being assigned to production. Once in production, a combination of peer pressure as well as supervisor monitoring serve as motivation for quality work. Some workers get flags by their work stations. A yellow flag means the worker has made one significant mistake in assembly; a red flag indicates two. If he makes a third one, he is moved into a job more in keeping with his capabilities. Reassignment, not firing, is the reaction to errors. This supports worker identification with the company and prevents the loss of training investment.

Lots of Rework, No Scrap

Samsung is one of the few Korean industries that has a significant system for documenting nonconformance. Executive Managing Director Y.M. Jung indicates that about 10% of the color TVs Samsung produces require some degree of rework. This is fairly comparable to rework rates at Sony in Japan. Of 1,800 refrigerators produced by Samsung, some 5% required rework. There was no scrap generated in either the TV or refrigerator line. In the microwave line — and Samsung claims to have about 13% of the U.S. market — they had 3 to 4% rework. Zero defects is the quality goal throughout the organization. Quality programs center around technology, vendor control, and personnel motivation.

Young Work Force

The average age of workers at Samsung is 20, and their annual bonus, based on longevity, averages about four months' pay. There is no union, but, as with POSCO, there is a management-labor council where elected workers meet with management to settle differences. Quality circles number between 400 and 500. They meet weekly on their own initiative. These circles set their own goals. When one set of goals is met, new goals are established. Total quality control is a way of life at Samsung.

Quality of Life Company Policy

At Samsung, the group chairman has established a three point corporate policy: to serve Korea through business, put human resources above material, and require efficient management. Samsung Electronics also has a four-point policy that encourages a quality of work life approach: cultivate mutual respect of all Samsung employes, create vitality throughout the organization, create an atmosphere of mutual trust, and complete all work to perfection.

It is easy to see why Samsung has been awarded the Korean Presidential Award for Quality.

ORIENTAL PRECISION CO., LTD.

Oriental Precision Co. (OPC) manufactures telecommunications and computer peripherals, portable field radio transceivers (PRC 77 and VRC 12), sonobuoys, traffic control systems, etc. The firm has a reliability testing system second to none. Here is a manufacturer confident enough of its design and manufacturing system to subject the product to shock and drop tests that truly duplicate the treatment communication gear is likely to receive in the battlefield.

Very education-minded, OPC is a major funder of Dae-Yeu Tech College, a local technical school which trains, among others, OPC personnel.

QUALITY: THE BALL IN YOUR COURT

Sound Organization

Kwang Hyun Kim, a retired general of the Republic of Korea Army, is president of OPC. He also identifies himself as the one responsible for quality control at OPC. "The QC director reports directly to me, as it must be," he says.

More than 189 quality circles involve 3,000 plus employes. Oriental Precision Company's three quality thrusts are: Ensuring employes are adequately trained and motivated, ensuring materials and vendor components meet customer specs, and checking final product to ensure it meets customer expectations. The middle point is particularly important, since OPC is assembly oriented, fabricating only 20% of its components locally.

GOLD STAR GUMI

In a remote southeastern region of Korea is Gold Star Gumi, a missile overhaul facility. The work spaces, even during full operation, are operating-room clean. Accurate rework figures for each type of missile are recorded: 4.6% rework on the Sidewinder, 5% on the I Hawk, and 3% on the Vulcan.

Interplant competition spurs Gumi's more than 60 quality circles to see which circle can generate the most significant ideas for improvement of quality or productivity. There is no union — only a management-labor council — and bi-annual bonuses amount to four and one-half months pay (equivalent to a total of nine months pay) paid out twice a year. Company housing and night school assistance promote company identity and support the theory that training and education promote quality and productivity.

KOREAN STANDARDS ASSOCIATION

The Korean Standards Association (KSA), created in 1962, pursues much the same path as JUSE. In 1971, it was designated as the training institute for certified quality engineers, and in 1977, it was named national headquarters for quality circles promotion.

KSA is headed by Jong Wan Choi, the executive vice president (also president of Hyo Sung Heavy Industries, Ltd.). Cho Jung-Wan serves as the action officer. The organization is composed of six departments, ranging from general affairs to quality control. Nine regional offices provide convenient operational locations. Between 1962 and 1982, unit membership (company = unit) grew from 95 to 1,431. And, in the organization's first 20 years, some 7,291 Korean industrial standards were published.

KSA offers 41 classes in eight basic subjects of quality, and 36,620 Koreans are graduates of those programs. These classes range from top management to worker level. In addition to promotion of quality circles and training, KSA organizes and supports international quality seminars and symposia. It publishes five periodicals and numerous quality books and training aids. Nearly 400 qualified experts in the field of quality provide consulting and training services. KSA claims that 20% of all workers in Korean industry are members of the country's 34,716 quality circles.

Like JUSE, KSA's strength lies in the fact that its membership consists of firms, not individuals. As a result, it can generate the financial backing and corporate interest in quality so essential for success of such a venture. Neither government action nor support from within the quality community can cause such an organization to be formed in the United States. The top management of U.S. corporations must bring this about. Any takers? The need does exist.

WHAT DO WE LEARN FROM KOREA?

Korea is an awakening industrial giant to be reckoned with in the near future. Survivors of a long and seesaw land war on their own homeland, they have demonstrated a singleness of purpose that demonstrates staying power. They have done a remarkable job of recovering from the war and now — enthusiastic and willing to work — are entering the world industrial competition arena. Taking a cue from their Japanese neighbor's success, they recognize that the key to success is quality.

Korea has several advantages over the United States and Europe. Some we can overcome with sufficient effort, others we cannot. One of the Korean advantages that won't disappear in the near future is its cheap labor pool. The wage difference may be reduced, but the traditional subsistence-level economy of Korea will continue to give Korean producers an edge. (An interesting point: There are no unemployment benefits in Korea. Families are expected to take care of their own.)

Education

While the Japanese focus on education is lauded in the Western world, Korea surpasses the Japanese in motivation and system. Japanese competition for admittance to colleges and universities is intense, but once there, many students coast. Not so in Korea. Although competition for college entry is as keen as it is in Japan, once in school, the attrition rate during freshman and sophomore years is significant. The Koreans believe that college is a place to learn and enhance one's value to the nation — not a social club at which future business friends may be cultivated. This education does not cease once out of technical school or college, but continues in off hours in one's chosen field.

QUALITY: THE BALL IN YOUR COURT

Work Ethic

Koreans are raised with the personal philosophy that hard work makes the difference. Instead of constantly looking for ways to shorten their work hours, days, or weeks, they believe God gave man his energy and strength to be used to conquer the problems he has either made for himself or fallen heir to through no fault of his own. Success, not leisure time, is the goal of a Korean, and success is measured by one's contribution to society. Koreans have no need for unions, for both management and labor have been weaned on the same work ethic. They can communicate with one another because they do not feel the need for a third party.

Management understands the contribution of labor as being the key to success and survival. Labor, accordingly, recognizes the contribution of management in providing capital, technology, and direction. It's a partnership arrangement rather than a competition.

Bonuses, company housing, schools, and recognition seem the appropriate way for management to recognize labor's contribution, and likewise, labor feels that an honest day's work is what an employer is entitled to and strives earnestly to give it to him.

Americans were born and flourished with the same understanding, but, since we've achieved success, we appear to have lost touch with honest, basic human relationships and worth.

Quality

Korean workers and managers recognize that consumers want quality *and value*. At the moment, constant, tedious rework is the means Koreans use to achieve that quality. But, having shown the capability to move out and achieve, the Koreans will soon learn that process control can give them an even greater edge in the international marketplace.

THE LESSON

Anyone who reads labels knows the incursions Korea has already made in the area of clothing, textiles, and shoes. "Made in Korea" does not signify inferior quality as "Made in Japan" did in the 1950s. Koreans have looked at Japan — their ancient conqueror and foe — and emulated their approach to quality.

The United States must analyze the factors that have contributed to Korea's success and emulate them. There are markets enough for all if we just take the trouble to develop them.

CHAPTER 8

ESSENTIAL ELEMENTS OF EXCELLENCE

There are eight elements that top management can use as a basic starting point in evaluating the focus the quality manager has established. Let's look at each area.

QUALITY TEAMS

Quality teams by edict may be productive since they sense the confidence management has in the system. First of all, do you have a quality team, or groups that resemble quality circles? If so, how many and how often do they meet? Do they meet on company time? Are they completely voluntary? Who's in charge, and what kind of agenda are they working from?

What's in it for the participant? Obviously the longevity and prosperity of the company is one commonly shared benefit, but is that all? How about the educational and cultural benefits? Have they been considered and advertised to the participants as benefits?

What do you expect out of the group and how will they document achievements? Do you have a reward and recognition system that is realistically based on cost avoidance, company savings, or greater profitability from increased productivity? Are the teams goal oriented and of manageable size? Does the team concept extend across disciplines? Did you begin the quality team process with a steering group to test the water? If so, have patience and wait for the dividends to arrive.

PROCESS CONTROL

For many years, each artificer felt a personal responsibility for the quality of his work. He identified with quality by putting his "mark" on the product, or if he was the only producer in the area, it was obvious who was accountable for the goods. Industrialization, mass production, and end-item inspection have eradicated that scene. Complexity, sophistication, and quantity of products has made direct accountability and identification unfeasible. Now, we must control the process to guarantee quality assurance.

Process control begins with the planning stage. It requires close interface with your customer and your design department during product formulation. The next step is determining what procedures will be used for process control of design, production, and quality. The best set of procedures is useless if it isn't understood and implemented by each worker.

To many, process control means no more inspection, but any new product will require at least a first-article inspection to ensure it meets specs, followed by a statistically sound spot-check thereafter. Defects uncovered as a result of these checks must be thoroughly analyzed to determine where and why the quality breakdown occurred. Control charts with upper and lower control limits must be established and monitored.

CORRECTIVE ACTION

Without corrective action, process control breaks down. People responsible for defects must be advised and redirected to preclude repetition of the error. Corrective action must be a team effort that includes design, engineering, production, and quality. If it involves purchased goods, it should include purchasing and the responsible vendor. It is essential that the corrective action have the ownership of all involved. Once the problem is analyzed and an acceptable solution has been derived, follow-up is necessary to assess the validity of the fix. If the problem has not been solved, back to the drawing board.

FACILITATION

The best training program and the most advanced engineering and design assets will avail little if your people are working with obsolete or inadequate equipment, a lack of floor space, or poor production flow layout. An efficient material control system and material requirements plan, an appropriate degree of automation, and an industrial environment that supports your quality standards are all essential elements of an acceptable facilitation plan.

One can't determine correspondence to customer specifications without accurate measurement. How accurate is your gaging instrumentation? The sophistication currently available in this phase of process control gives little excuse for ever having problems in this area. However, the best, most sophisticated measurement system is useless without an effective calibration system with a built-in audit safeguard.

Facilitation also calls for qualified supervisors who spend time on the floor — not in their comfortable cubbyholes. Most workers will utilize a supervisor when questions or problems arise, but not if the supervisor is not readily available.

An often overlooked adjunct to facilitation is employes' support and recreational facilities. Decent and adequately equipped restrooms, lounges, and eating facilities are not luxuries in today's society. They are expected. They help to identify a company that cares about its employes. The cost is minimal when compared to the potential payback.

TRAINING

Training is an exceedingly important factor in achieving high quality standards. For less complex operations, hands-on training may suffice, but, for best results, formal training is desirable. This is particularly true when significant modernization or update occurs.

One of the best insurance policies against demoralizing and quality-costly layoffs is to institute cross-skill training. Then, when sickness, vacation, or a market valley occurs, workers can be shifted to meet the skill demand. Marvin Runyon, president and general manager of Nissan America, has done this at Nissan's Smyrna, Tennessee plant. Workers who are cross-trained are paid at a higher scale than those who are not, but there is never a slow down on the production line due to a lack of skill.

Technology updates for supervisors and management are also important to nurture an attitude of constant improvement within your organization. The Japanese have discovered that mid-life training at age 45 does wonders in rejuvenating middle- and upper-level management.

QUALIFICATION/CERTIFICATION PROGRAMS

Qualification and certification programs with regularly scheduled audits ensure that personnel are indeed qualified. Such systems are particularly essential if the skills in question are of an extremely technical or exotic nature.

QUALITY STANDARDS

There are four gages by which to evaluate the realistic value of quality standards. First, they must be definable. If it is zero defects you'd like to establish as your house standard, by all means do so. Perhaps you prefer Deming's approach of constant improvement. Whatever the goal, have it clearly understood that this is *the* acceptable goal for everyone. Second, ensure that your people understand your published quality standard and be certain that this standard is measurable (gage three). If you have not opted for a zero defects standard, you should define as gage four the degree of nonconformance you are willing to accept. A base line is necessary to determine a starting point from which to measure progress. If you can't measure it, you can't manage it.

Recognize or reward workers who achieve the standard. If the standard has been jointly established by management and nonmanagement, the probability of its acceptance is increased by a hundredfold. If your standard had been established as less than zero defects, steadily raise the bars, just as you would in training a hurdler or high-jumper.

Somerset Maugham, the great English novelist, is quoted as having said, "It's a funny thing about life — if you refuse to accept anything but the best, you very often get it." Don't be timid in setting high standards. Your employes will rise to the occasion if you exemplify those same high standards of performance.

COMMUNICATION

Quality is largely a matter of effective communications between people. It must first be communicated, understood, and accepted in house. Part of the message must be the personal satisfaction quality will give every participant.

Next, communicate quality to your customers via the product or service you produce or provide. "Your product speaks so loudly, I can't hear what your advertising campaign is saying." The Edsel is an example of that truth — customers spoke with their pocketbooks. Buick's boast, "Ask the man who owns one," and Sears', "Satisfaction guaranteed" are long-lasting reminders of the customer satisfaction provided by their products.

It is also essential that stockholders and directors understand what quality means to their investment. Overall product integrity is essential for the reputation of your company and product in the marketplace and industry.

CHAPTER 9

QUALITY OF LIFE

How important are people to you? Are they to be used only as long as they require a minimum investment of time and money and then let go when they become marginally profitable or an expense? Do you update employes' technological skills or do you view retraining as a needless expense? Perhaps you say, "We'll just hire people fresh out of tech junior college. They must be up on all these new machines and procedures." Are people as important to you as automation or robotics? Do people have a future in your organization, or do you feel their constant wage and fringe increases and noncommensurate productivity increases are unwarranted expenses?

Peter Drucker, one of America's foremost management experts, in *Concept of the Corporation*, puts people into a proper context as he writes, "Modern production, and especially modern mass production, is not based on raw materials or gadgets, but on principles of organization . . . not of machines, but of human beings . . . ."[1]

THE HUMAN ELEMENTS OF QUALITY

One does not experience a successful exposure session, one does not imbue workers with a sense of mission, and one does not establish a positive corporate image if management and labor don't function in an atmosphere of mutual respect. Are management and nonmanagement a team in your company, or is there an "us-them" rivalry that prevents everyone from turning out quality? Are the professionals considered to be the elite of the work force, while the molder, the pattern maker, the lathe operator, welder, and assembler are necessary evils to be tolerated but not venerated?

If the latter is the case, consider from whence cash flow is generated. From drawings, or from completed product? From management techniques, or from delivered goods? Salaried and hourly workers must cooperate to furnish quality to consumers.

Leaders and Followers

Leadership is another important element. It is perhaps the most misunderstood and, thus, poorly taught element in management schools today. Leadership is the thoroughbred who leads the pack to the finish line. Management is the draught horse who dutifully makes the rounds, routinely and profitably delivering beer kegs to the customers. This is not to disparage the talents or contributions of managers. They make the bottom line black each reporting period. They stimulate growth, but seldom do they inspire people to work above what they feel are their limitations. And that ability to inspire is what leadership is all about: causing people to live beyond their imagined limitations — getting them to reach beyond "good enough" and discover their true potentials for quality or productivity. It is essential that a good manager also be a good leader if he desires the establishment of a quality culture within his firm.

Equally important in a quality of life program is the need for dedicated followers — not followers of the sort who followed Jim Jones into oblivion in Guyana, but those who can question without being disloyal; those who give their best efforts and inspire others to do likewise. Not everyone can be a leader, but everyone can learn to be a dedicated follower.

Responsibility and accountability. Does all responsibility reside on top and middle managements' shoulders, or has it been distributed throughout the organization? The manager who tries to handle all details himself will damage his effectiveness as a quality manager. Besides, delegation of responsibility stimulates growth and job satisfaction. It increases the self-assurance and pride workers need to feel their contributions to the firm are important and worthy of their best efforts.

The Siamese twin of responsibility is accountability, a leadership characteristic widely neglected in recent decades. Companies fail or lose money, and the decision makers who were paid to know better are quietly reassigned or allowed to float softly on a no-penalty golden parachute. If we are ever to establish a quality society, we must upgrade the importance of accountability of all hands.

Goals and self-improvement. Goals are also important in a quality of life program. Are your company goals well known and supported? Did your workers have any input in establishing them? Does everyone believe the goals to be achievable, desirable, and of value to him or her personally? If so, there's a better than even chance you will get support for those goals. If they are vague, if they were created in a vacuum, or if they're viewed as unrealistic, your chances of support are greatly reduced.

Self-improvement is an absolute necessity when we consider a quality of life program. This can be achieved by in-house sponsored training or education and by motivating people to improve themselves on their own time. The motivation for this must be clearly defined as promotional opportunity within your company.

Obviously, education will also improve an employe's external employment value. But, it is up to you to emphasize the employe's new opportunity to move up *within* the corporation.

Team Spirit is Inspirational

The idea of belonging to a winning team is inspirational and infectious. When the Redskins, Steelers, or Cowboys bring home the Super Bowl trophy, everyone in the hometown suddenly becomes "one of the team," and it is hard to resist joining the "We're number one" chant. In industry, it is difficult to be a winner without that team spirit.

Individual and Corporate Identity

People like to feel that they are important. One way managers can give that feeling is to learn their workers' names. The cost of this employe benefit is zero; the payback is in mutual respect and the increased effort of happy employes.

Of almost equal importance is the employes' identification with their employer. There are three keys to cultivating such an identity lock.

Key one. Encourage interpersonal relationships. Schedule exposure sessions to update your people on plans, achievements, problems, and potentials, and make yourself available to field their questions. The latter element can be painful because this generation is not reluctant to dethrone authority. On the other hand, such sessions provide a great catharsis for employes who may need a frustration outlet to restore morale. Restrain your anger, flip answers, biting sarcasm, or the perfect put-down, however tempted you may be to snap back. You are on the firing line to determine just how *cool* an operator you really are. If you're unsure of the answer to a question or plain don't know, admit it. Promise to find out and get back with an answer. No one knows everything about everything, nor is he or she expected to. These questions may make you aware of areas about which you should be more knowledgeable.

Key two. Sell your people on the importance of what they do. As Douglas D. Danforth, chairman of Westinghouse, says, "Our performance in the marketplace will be determined by quality as the customer perceives it. It does not matter whether it is product performance, service, competitive pricing, responsiveness to customer needs, or just answering a phone call. Every service you render pushes the enterprise up. Every disservice pushes it down. Too many people think that high quality always carries a high price tag. Wrong."[2]

Is yours an insurance business? Is it just a means of separating people from their money, or does it provide a service people *need* in order to cope with the uncertainties of life and to make provisions for their survivors?

Perhaps you are making automobiles or automotive components. Your people must be made to identify their work as important in the provision of mobility for the

85

public. The job isn't the installation of a right front-disc brake — it's satisfying the public's need for safe and reliable transportation. *That* is a mission that demands a worker's best efforts and full attention.

Key three. The third important key is the company's public identity. Is it positive? Do people outside of Podunk, where your main (perhaps only) plant is located, know about the FGH Automatic Can Opener Mfg. Co.? Corporate identity is second only to the reputation of your products. Corporate image, like product reputation, is built on quality. Both involve close correspondence between real virtue and advertising claims.

Perhaps your corporation is so diversified that its reputation and reputations of its products have long seemed separate. Be slow to draw that conclusion. Consumers are aware of companies that enjoy long and virtuous reputations. The automobile industry has painfully learned the price one pays for trading the reputation birthright for market indifference.

FUN IS FUNDAMENTAL TO SUCCESS

Would you rather be doing what you're doing than anything else? If not, why continue?

As Don Farrar, president of Avco Operations, Textron, Inc., asks, "Why is it that we have so little dedication and enthusiasm for efforts on which we spend almost one third of our lives and half our waking hours?"

The answer most often is, we're not having fun. Work should be a joy, and it can be if we create an environment that causes people to look forward to work. Following are ideas for restoring zest and identity to the workplace.

Universal Contribution

• Develop a positive mental attitude (PMA). If you find you don't approach each day saying, as PMA speaker Ed Foreman does, "It's gonna be a *gooood* day," then move on. Don't spend your life being miserable in your work.

• Get to know your fellow employes. Use your coffee break to extend your opportunity for fellowship and positive influence.

• Consider the future of the company as *your* future. Make it a bright one.

• Give every job you do your best shot. Don't waste your time on shoddy effort.

• Consider your time as your only unrecyclable treasure. Make it count. Use time wisely.

• Participate in company programs and activities. Join the team and help it make a winning effort.

• Bear in mind, scrap and rework have no reward for the company or you. Do your best to do it right the first time every time.

• When in doubt, ask your supervisor. Don't muddle through because you are too shy or embarrassed to ask for help.

• Identify with the company. It represents not only your livelihood, but your future growth and opportunity.

• Strive for constant improvement as your prime contribution to that winning team to which you belong.

• Demonstrate respect for your subordinates' personalities. They're living, breathing humans who are unique in their responses to stimuli. Learn what evokes a positive response from them.

• Maintain an open channel of communication with superiors and subordinates. Keep everyone informed of what's going on so nobody feels he or she is a "mushroom."

• Know what's going on. Stay out on the floor with your eyes and ears open. Manage by walking around.

• Praise in public, reprimand in private. Never miss an opportunity to "catch someone doing something right," as *The One-Minute Manager* advises. If your subordinates are fouled up either through ignorance or indifference, don't hesitate to bring this to their attention, but in private, not before their peers.

• Tangibily demonstrate interest in your subordinates' welfare. If they've got personal problems, take time to counsel or provide a sympathetic ear. So it makes you late getting home from work. Shouldn't their problems be yours if listening helps them become a more responsible and grateful team member?

• Lead by example. Don't expect your people to demonstrate team spirit if you are always knocking your superiors in management. If you are a late-in, early-out supervisor, how can you reprimand tardiness on the part of your people?

• Promote company identity programs. This is essential if you want a winning team.

• Take the drudgery out of work. Make work as much fun as possible for all, yourself included. Encourage humor and interaction on the job.

• Provide an orientation program for all new employees. Where possible, include spouses. They are extremely important in promoting a positive quality of life environment.

• Provide formal training for both white-and blue-collar employes. This should include periodic refresher training that updates employes technically and in product awareness.

• Develop a favorable physical environment. Consider cleanliness, orderliness, and appointments in your own office and in other work spaces. Update and improve lunch areas, lounges, and restrooms. It's amazing what a small investment in these areas will gain you.

• Provide an environment of job security.

• Develop and implement a plan to stimulate loyalty to the corporation, the division, and the section.

• Identify "up-comers" with great potential and invest the time to develop their potential. Don't promote prematurely, throwing people into positions they're not yet ready to assume.

• Promote from within. Avoid going outside to fill key slots, as much as possible.

• Develop a good worker reward system as a satisfactory alternative to promotion.

• Provide periodic refresher training for executives.

• Structure bonuses to reward above-and-beyond effort, not just long and faithful service.

MANAGEMENT'S IMPACT ON QUALITY OF LIFE

There are three principal quality of life areas a manager can affect within his realm of authority and responsibility: attitude, discipline, and resources. You, as a general manager, are uniquely capable of impacting these areas more than anyone else.

Attitude Orientation

How can you balance the cost of people and their productivity? The key is attitude orientation.

Without question, the most critical change necessary to achieve a quality culture, is the changing of peoples' attitudes about what they do. To change attitudes, one must first define quality. Does it mean excellence? To excel? Does quality mean there is none better? Actually, no. It means fulfilling the customer's expectations and having a fitness for use. A Volkswagen can and should represent quality as much as a Rolls Royce, Mercedes, or Jaguar — depending on the taste and purse of the customer. Quality is doing the right thing right, the first time, on time, and achieving value in the buyers' eyes. Concomitantly, there must be profit to the seller or production capability will soon disappear.

All who have anything to do with design, manufacture, sales, or service must perceive themselves as owning responsibility for this quality. This, together with a performance standard that covers the spectrum of product or service creation, will ensure a mindset that supports your quality culture.

Our complex society is overwhelmed by the negative messages of the news media and is constantly reminded that the nuclear sword of Damocles hangs over the human race. It is little wonder that we no longer associate quality with giving our best efforts in all we do. The moral absolutes of the Bible have given way to situational ethics, and the only sin is to get caught. We pay our entertainers on the stage or playing field more than we do our president or legislators, and then wonder why the best-qualified people aren't drawn to run for public office.

Our cynicism regarding basic tenets such as honesty, integrity, and commitment spawns "get-by" efforts, clock-watching dedication, shoddy work, and litigation for perceived employment bias. Is it any wonder we have a quality problem in this nation?

The attitude problem is not restricted to "them." It is "us" also. Sensing the possibility of a board's dissatisfaction with our future efforts, or a possible hostile takeover, we negotiate golden parachutes into our contracts, giving ourselves a sense of security and reducing our need to be competitive.

We blame others for the problems our company suffers: "Union work rules have ruined the worker." "Workers now expect fringes that are out of sight, and they feel no sense of responsibility for judicious use of medical or dental care." "Productivity has fallen off and overtime occasioned by rework and repair is creating a real morale problem."

We continue to call in consultants and specialists to identify problems and forgo the management responsibility which is patently ours. If people are our problem, then it's *our* responsibility to learn how to work with them. If poor morale is killing quality and productivity, management must create an environment that will enhance morale and cause people to feel that coming to work for the ABC Company is the most exciting, challenging, and rewarding thing they can do. Pipe dream? Absolutely not. It is definitely achievable. Later in this chapter you will find a few suggestions on methods.

Discipline Essential

System discipline is an essential element in exacting efficiency and effectiveness. It is a self-discipline that says, "What *I* do is important to quality." It is much easier to assign others the responsibility for quality and downplay one's own contribution.

QUALITY: THE BALL IN YOUR COURT

A quality culture must begin as a conscious responsibility of each individual in the organization.

This discipline must flow from the top and permeate every production process. Statistical quality control must be a way of life in every critical process of the manufacturing procedure. Discipline in design, purchasing, vendor relationships, marketing, and service departments — all must operate within clearly stated rules and regulations that lend discipline and predictability to the system, but which don't stifle creativity, initiative, or innovation.

Organizational discipline is based on every party's recognition of the mutually reinforcing importance of the quality triangle of producer, vendor, and customer. Each makes a vital contribution to the success of any quality improvement process. The vendor supplies specs that meet user-requirement parts on time and at price. The producer manufactures and assembles the product correctly the first time, thereby giving his customer the lowest price, thereby making a profit and sustaining competitive advantage. The customer, the remaining side of this triad, feeds back his approval or disapproval to the producer, providing sufficient detail to allow correction or improvement of the product. Without this feedback, the producer may live in a fool's paradise, believing his product or service is acceptable when, in fact, it is not.

Resources

An inescapable top management responsibility is the prudent assignment of resources. Of equal truth is the fact that, without resources, little of a positive nature occurs.

But, isn't quality free? Yes and no. If we do the right thing right the first time — what we pay our employes for and for which we are paid — and produce an acceptable product or service at the lowest possible cost, in that case quality is indeed free. However, in a culture that has not yet focused on quality as a way of worklife, we need to reform mindsets, and changing a culture is indeed an expensive undertaking. The alternative, of course, is to fall farther behind in competitiveness.

Perhaps the most critical resource a top manager can supply is time — time to participate actively as the leader in the move to a quality culture in one's organization. It is amazing the effect a manager's active participation in the quality improvement process can have on his or her subordinates. Vice presidents, directors, managers, foremen, and first-line supervisors generally take interest in a manager's interests. If a manager's interest is limited to lip service rather than involvement, subordinates' participation will be likewise. Ergo, time is the most valuable contribution a manager can make.

Commitment of resources to provide adequate training and re-training, to provide equipment capable of holding the tolerances your product demands, or to provide efficient office equipment, uses your employe's time to best competitive advantage. Are your facilities designed to accommodate your current production or customer schedule? Have you recently checked to ensure your production flow avoids back or cross-tracking as various sequential functions are performed? Have you ignored your industrial engineers' admonitions to expand or update equipment to meet quality and production standards? Have you used the oft-heard excuse, "I can't afford it now. When business gets better, I'll modernize?" You may not remain in a position for business to get better with that attitude.

How about expertise on the floor, in design, engineering, or marketing? Do you have any kind of executive training program that keeps those functions up-to-date with the times, technology, and competition? Expertise can be even more important than facilities or equipment.

Recognition

As a final thought about management's impact on quality of life, how about tangible recognition in the form of gain sharing or bonuses for your employes? After all, are they not responsible for your business success? What motivation do they have for making your business more successful and more competitive? Why not share a piece of the pie? If employes feel they are just making the effort for you, your executive staff, and your shareholders, their effort will be less than it would if they felt they'd profit from extra effort and care.

Recognition is an important element in any quality of life enhancement program. This recognition can take place simply by walking through the shop area and getting acquainted with the work force. This can mean the difference between your success or failure as a manager. It can be an all-hands meeting at which a more formal acknowledgment can be made. It can be a trophy, a bonus, or a handshake. What it must be is management's acknowledgement of a job superbly done, commensurate with established quality standards: meaningful recognition.

In all of this, there must be a feeling of mutual trust and respect. Promised rewards and benefits must also be honored. If there is any hint of management compromise on either standards or performance evaluation, your program of recognition and reward for performance will disintegrate.

Too often, management and labor have imagined that money is the only recognition — that, in lieu of respect, cash settlements will buy off frazzled nerves, inattention to detail, adversarial emotions, etc. This bribery fails to produce quality because it fails to produce teamwork, self-respect, or competency. Instead it produces a rift in the day's-work-for-a-day's-pay connection. It produces a spiraling wage rate and a work force that is motivated by dollars, not deeds.

QUALITY: THE BALL IN YOUR COURT

To Change a Culture

Changing a culture is not easy. Habits, traditions, and mindsets are slow to change. Culture change requires education, example, and proper recognition to be successful. One short training session will not do it. Repetition and reiteration must include not only the "whats" of quality, but also the "whys." Perhaps the best teaching asset is one's own example of excellence in all activities. An environment of job security helps greatly. A plant that stimulates loyalty to the division or corporation will help create the ownership or identity that will make employe attitudes positive toward what they do.

If you identify "comers" and assist them to achieve their potential, you'll signal your interest in people, and promoting from within squelches the feeling that everything good comes from the outside. Consider how promoting from within stimulates competition among and effort from those whose loyalty and dedication has already been established. Development of an award system for outstanding workers can be used as a satisfactory alternative to promotion when advancement opportunities stagnate.

Can excellence be achieved in industry today? Can the United States regain its reputation for quality? Absolutely. It requires only People, Professionalism, Resources, Identity, Dedication, and Enthusiasm. Put them together and they spell PRIDE — pride in workmanship and pride in belonging.

In speaking about how to obtain quality of life, Sir William Osler said, "Live neither in the past nor the future, but let each day's work absorb all your interest, energy, and enthusiasm. The best preparation for tomorrow is to do today's work superbly well."[3]

Amen!

Footnotes

1. Peter F. Drucker, *Concept of the Corporation* (Boston, Mass.: Beacon Press, 1960), p. 213.
2. Douglas D. Danforth, "Quality Means Doing the Job Right the First Time," *Newsweek*, 30 Jan. 1984, p. 10.
3. Harvey Cushing, *Life of Sir William Osler* (Oxford: Clarendon, 1925).

CHAPTER 10

PROBLEM SOLVING

IN OR OUT OF HOUSE?

"There are no problems, only challenges and opportunities."

John Wayne may never be superseded as an American folk hero. His manly physique, thoughtful drawl, polite respect for ladies and elders, honesty, open patriotism and sincerity, not to mention his quick draw and deadly aim, captured the imagination of generation after generation who fantasized him as the person they would most like to be. Unfortunately, generations of managers have emulated The Duke's quick-draw, shoot-from-the-hip approach to their companies' more complex problems. "Just bring the varmints to me, ma'am [or sir], and I'll shoot them right out of the saddle. After all, ain't that what I'm hired to do?"

The answer is a resounding "No." The president, vice president, or general manager is hired to manage resources and to stimulate and lead people. This implies the highest degree of coordination and inspiration.

It is the manager's responsibility to see that professional and technical talent are in place and then, like a symphony conductor, to orchestrate that talent to please the customers.

Problem solving must involve everyone in the corporation in some way or another. It cannot be a one-man show. Any manager who is jealous of his subordinates' efforts to make the company a success does not deserve the title of manager. No one in corporate life who considers himself a loner is qualified to wear a white hat.

Managers must recognize talent and have the insight and skill to coordinate that talent to produce a winning team. They exploit the strengths and versatility of their people to produce the synergy of success. They must have the perception to hire and the guts to fire. They look at ways to bring out the best in each member of their teams. They down play rivalries that lead to dissension, but encourage competition that causes people to work beyond themselves. They "raise the bars," so, like Olympic contenders, their team members are not satisfied with equalling records — they're out to break them.

QUALITY: THE BALL IN YOUR COURT

Far too often and for too long, managers have barricaded themselves in their well-appointed offices. They don't know the actual extent of their organizations' problems, nor have they mobilized their best problem solvers. Their withdrawal has been so complete that the phrase, "management by walking around," has recently been regarded as something of a revolutionary concept.

For those who await the identification of a problem by a subordinate while the boss sits on his throne, the wait will be a long one. Not that subordinates deliberately desire to scuttle their own economic survival vessel — it's just that they've learned not to disturb the boss who's sharpening his putting eye in an oak-panelled office. Also, each instance of a bruised and bleeding messenger discourages news bearing.

Directors as Problem Solvers

It is sometimes assumed that corporate directors can function in place of management as problem solvers. This misses the mark. Directors' contributions lie in the area of approving or disapproving management's decisions about expansion, divestiture, debt increase, election of corporate officers, response to proposals, new product undertaking, reaction to hostile takeover attempts, and the like. They aren't appropriate day-to-day fire fighters.

Intelligent managers recognize their own limitations and delegate much of the problem-solving responsibility to their own top staffs, but they don't subtract themselves from the process. They require problems to be brought to their attention and may themselves offer comments or alternatives. In other words, the intelligent manager is neither a lone gun nor one who washes his hands of a problem.

Exploring the Problem-Solving Bank

At Tohoku Nitsuko Ltd., a telephone equipment manufacturing company near Tokyo, a sign reads: "The first rule of the job is to have an inquiring mind." Consider the potential problem identification such an invitation carries. It welcomes employes to question, among other things, company procedures and policies. Nitsuko increases that potential through an active suggestion program. The benefit of full participation is that the "extra" problem solvers, as a group, have much more knowledge of plan or production problems than any executive or group of executives can possibly supply.

T. Fuji, managing director of Nitsuko states, "We are not manufacturing telephone equipment, but quality." Quality teams, coupled with well-administered programs, have been a rich source of new ideas and solutions to long-festering problems, and they cement a quality partnership between management and workers.

The Role of Consultants

If you have neither the talent nor initiative within your organization to identify or organize the elements of your quality problem, the professional quality or management consultant can contribute. The solution, however, is yours alone.

The consultant, through structured interface with *your* people, attempt to identify your quality problem. Be forewarned that most problems will be management related, since that is where policy is made and resources managed.

Depending on the consultant's professional experience and persuasion, the package delivered will be the identification of *your* problems. It will draw on *your* suggestions. Perhaps even the solutions will be yours. Surely it will be you who determines and implements recommendations and corrective actions.

If you decide you're ready and willing to address your problems in-house, consider the following eight approaches. They're guaranteed to make you and your team more able.

ISHIKAWA FISHBONE DIAGRAM

The fishbone approach to problem solving is an interactive exercise that requires a facilitator and is normally worked on during company time by quality circles. Perfected by Kaoru Ishikawa, the fishbone approach is a three-step process.

Step one. Group participants identify elements they feel have the most impact on quality (see Figure 10-1). For the sake of illustration, let's consider eight areas: competence, commitment, responsiveness/adaptability, continuous improvement, quality of product, safety, cost/productivity, and market strategy/niche. These are by no means all-inclusive (see Figure 10-2).

Step two. To flesh out the fishbone, we identify elements that fall within each of these areas. For instance, how can management influence *competence*? Is the establishment of performance standards significant in developing competence? How about supervision? Can it influence your personnel's feeling of security in knowing what is expected? Does performance appraisal reinforce such counsel? How about promotion? Does it motivate or demotivate? Does your education and training system reflect your concern for quality through the development of competent workers and managers?

Consider *commitment*. Do employes feel that they have equity in the company? Do they proudly identify with the source of their income? What types of rewards and shared futures do they see? Do these stimulate their commitment to quality?

How about *responsiveness* to customers' requirements and adaptability to market changes? Do schedule considerations take precedence over quality? Would a flexible machining system improve responsiveness and market adaptability? To

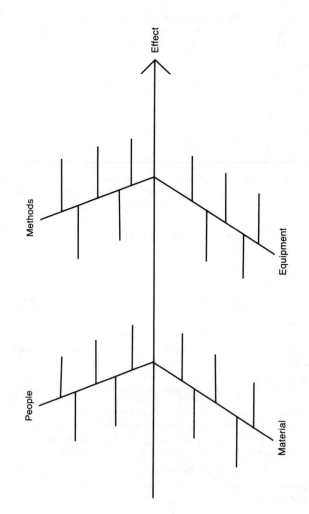

Model Fishbone Diagram

Figure 10-1

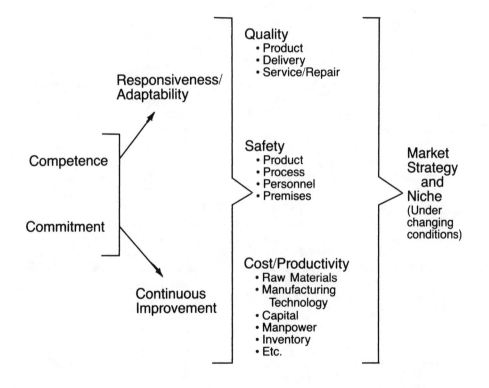

Figure 10-2

97

what degree do your marketers have their fingers on the pulse of the market? Are you investing any funds in R&D in order to *influence* the market?

Is there a recognizable attitude of *continuous improvement* in your organization? If not, how can you create one? What kind of suggestion program do you have, and how active and effective is it? Does customer feedback figure in this element?

Does your *quality system* encompass product delivery, service/tech reps? How about job satisfaction? Does your quality of work life process promote job satisfaction? How do you achieve process control? Is your vendors' quality assured? Do you have company-wide total quality control?

Do you have a functioning *safety* program? Are all hands involved? Do you understand the contributions it makes toward quality, productivity, and quality of work life? Do you publish an accident evaluation to avoid repetitions? What kind of recognitions and rewards do you offer for safety improvement suggestions?

Perhaps the most important area to survey is the cost of *production*. How much is poor design costing in engineering design changes? Is inventory management in hand? Do you have a just-in-time system that relies on vendors to deliver conforming parts when promised? Are nonconformance costs (often mislabled "cost of quality") known, and are they acceptably low?

Is quality a factor in your *marketing strategy*? How do your customers compare you with your competitors? Is your firm working on new product innovations? How successful have you been in disseminating an acceptance of the strategy within your organization? Who does your strategic quality planning? How do you determine market niche? What is your advertising and awareness strategy?

Step three. Major problem areas have been identified and forces listed that have impact on those areas. Now top management must demonstrate the degree of participation it intends to have in establishing a quality culture. How many problem areas can be pursued economically? Which problem should be tackled first and which should follow to establish a logical flow of improvement? If you are a division, how will corporate coordinate resources to inspire initiative and prevent bias?

CEDAC

Ryuji Fukuda, an international quality authority, author of *Managerial Engineering* (published by Productivity, Inc.) and consultant to the Meidensha Electric Manufacturing Company, has devised a tool he labels a "cause-and-effect diagram with the addition of cards" (CEDAC). It uses the Ishikawa fishbone diagram and control chart to display a problem and its scope (see Figure 10-3). Employes are invited to consider a problem and add cards suggesting causes and solutions. Management harvests the cards daily and evaluates them, assuring recognition to all participants. This appears to have great merit. For more detail on CEDAC, read Fukuda's excellent treatise. It's one of the best new quality references published.

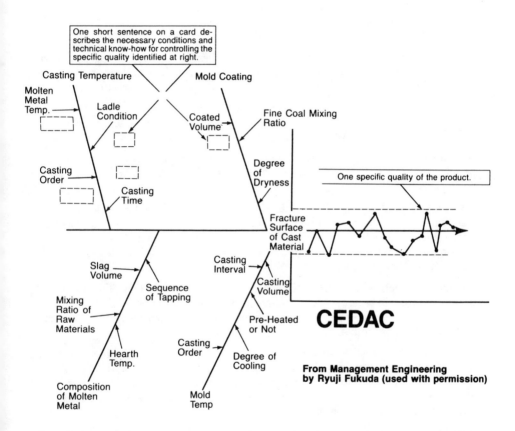

Figure 10-3

99

BRAINSTORMING — OR NOMINAL GROUP EFFORT

What a revelation it is when management discovers brainstorming. This nominal group effort is a basic and ad hoc way to identify available talent and utilize it in identifying and solving problems. It will boost quality and productivity and provide your workers with the satisfaction and professional growth they deserve. It begins with a group of people. They can be homogeneous or heterogeneous and in any of the criteria by which you classify your people — i.e., hourly, salaried, professional, technical, management, educational, and so forth.

Step one. A few days before calling the group together, describe the problem you hope to clearly identify. Quantify it and develop a plan of action. This will give participants the opportunity to become mentally attuned to the subject you wish to address.

Step two. As a corporate body, describe the problem in detail to the assembled group, and allow participants to ask any questions that will better establish the limits of the problem. Allow no suggestions at this point.

Step three. The silent generation. This is a quiet time of reflection that allows people time to think about any new dimensions the problem description might have generated.

Step four. Round robin. The expression of ideas begins. Ground rules must be stated and inflexibly enforced by the facilitators. They are: proceed around a circle person by person, allowing each person to express only one thought per round. If a person cannot come up with an input, he or she should pass. This does not obviate an input on the next turn.

An alternate method is to let people describe ideas spontaneously. This permits a person to throw in several ideas simultaneously. The rotation method, on the other hand, ensures that no one is left out or intimidated into silence by the more vocal and enthusiastic members.

No comments should be made by the facilitator or any member regarding the quality or appropriateness of any suggestion at this point. Humor and exaggeration are to be encouraged. No suggestion will be thrown out or combined with another at this point. A scribe will write out each suggestion on easel-mounted butcher paper to stimulate synergistic piggybacking.

Step five. At the end of a set time (or, if time isn't a factor, when the well has run dry), the editing and discussion phase begins. At this time, misunderstandings are resolved and ideas better defined. Some of the input may be consolidated, if that's appropriate. At this time also, you may want to group related ideas.

Step six. The facilitator at this point asks members to vote on each idea on the refined list as to which ideas will be useful in solving the problem and which will not. Members may vote on as many ideas as they desire.

Step seven. Consensus. Ideas deemed unlikely to be useful should not be discarded. Some may be diamonds in the rough. In the consensus phase, each member of the brainstorming group votes for only one idea. The purpose here is to reduce the final menu to an acceptable scope.

Step eight. Having harvested the best ideas and reduced them to a manageable menu, ascertain their relative merits. Which are practicable from a resource standpoint? Which are likely to produce the most results? Now assign responsibility for implementation — who will be in charge and who assists and supports.

Step nine. An essential element in brainstorming is to follow up with a plan of action derived by corporate effort. It is essential to establish that this is a serious undertaking and also to ensure that needed resources are made available.

QUALITY CIRCLES

Quality circles can identify problems, verify the validity of a problem, gather data to support the contention, brainstorm the cause, collect supporting data, brainstorm the solution, verify its validity, and determine cost and value gained before presenting all this to management for approval and implementation. In addition, they offer a wide scope for employe action. Circles can address such issues as quality, efficiency, productivity, and cost reduction; they can work on topics like facility planning, tool design, production control, administrative procedures, service/product image enhancement, and customer relations. In short, quality circles can solve problems.

The first step in forming a circle is for a manager to convince subordinates in influential positions of the value of quality circles. This is best achieved by forming a quality circle steering group. The group is composed of 10 to 12 employes from a spectrum of disciplines and pay levels.

Be objective as you describe what quality circles are and what they can and can't do for the organization. Encourage discussion and don't arbitrarily silence dissenters. Give them full opportunity to air their objections and biases. Use practical examples within your organization to establish the need and potential for circles. Specify some of the goals you believe quality circles will achieve when implemented. Benefits include:

- Raising the status of employes.
- Exploiting workers' accumulated wisdom and creativity.
- Helping individual development.
- Unifying the group.
- Achieving mutual education.
- Recognition of workers' achievements.
- Giving employes a sense of ownership.
- Giving employes an incentive to do better.

QUALITY: THE BALL IN YOUR COURT

Describe the training that equips facilitators, leaders, and members. Be candid, show no impatience, and don't try to ramrod the concept through. Without true consensus, quality circles will die aborning.

Having successfully sold the steering group on quality circles (which may be quite enough for the first session), schedule a meeting to set up a plan of action, establish milestones, and assign responsibility. This important phase will help preclude premature stalemate and ensure a logical sequence of events. This plan will include, but not be limited to, the number of circles, membership (voluntary or total), quality circles policy, "off-limit" topics, a training plan, selection of facilitators, and the initial method of leader selection (e.g., will it be the current supervisor or another management selection?).

The second most important aspect of assuring success in quality circles is to make sure training is varied and comprehensive. There are a number of consultants who, taking advantage of the quality mania now extant, will offer to train your group. Exercise due caution in making a selection. Training that is too short will sacrifice depth and will leave facilitators and quality circle leaders uncertain about their ability to fulfill their roles. The Quality Circle Institute is a group that has solid credentials in this business.

Concomitant with training of facilitators and leaders should be a publicity campaign to prepare your constituents for what's about to happen. With such preparation, the culture shock will be greatly reduced. The head person should be in the first facilitators' class if he or she has the time, for that learning experience, too, will be valuable.

Problem solving via quality circles is one of the most exciting and profitable experiences you will ever have, regardless of how many degrees you have earned. In addition, it establishes a fantastic degree of credibility with your people. If you can run your entire steering group through the training, you can really assure the success of quality circles. The facilitators in turn train prospective leaders.

When facilitator and leader training is complete, you are ready to begin quality control circle (QCC) training. Yes, each member of each QCC will receive essentially the same introduction to engineered problem-solving techniques. After three sessions of training, your circles can begin preliminary problem-solving at a place and time provided by management. (Eight sessions completes the set.)

To get circles started on the right foot, consider "seeding" the groups with initial discussion/study/problem areas. And consider having management show interest by *unobtrusively* listening in on initial meetings — but be sure to avoid the appearance of management control.

Data Collection and Display

One of the strong points of the quality circle approach to problem solving is the fact that, prior to determining the cause of a problem, the circle must verify via data that this *is* a problem and the extent to which it affects efficiency, productivity, quality, and so forth. This data is accumulated through various processes.

Initially, a checklist should be established to determine the type or nature of data needed to support the validity of the problem. Checklists are used by virtually everyone — by housewives to ensure efficient grocery shopping, by campers to ensure that all gear is present before weighting anchor, and by pilots to ensure that takeoffs and landings will come out evenly. Check sheets, on the other hand, are used to *compile* data (i.e., number of widgets not meeting specs on the first shift, or number of customer returns experienced from a certain lot of merchandise delivered) (see Figure 10-4). Drawings and photographs are another source of data which is used in problem solving and can be used subsequently in a management presentation.

An aspect of QCCs almost as important as training is the management presentation phase. (The term "management" as it is used here refers to whatever level has the authority to approve the proposal.) This is the time when the circle presents the solutions to the problem either you or they have identified. At such a presentation, I would suggest the "three be's" of success: be present, be responsive, and be appreciative — otherwise, you may demotivate the group, and once it hits the general telegraph that the boss really isn't with quality circles, look out. You've just laid a bomb.

Two more for management. First, emphasize interest by providing resources, recognition, and reward to circles, and by participating. Second, don't expect instant acceptance of the circle concept — or instant results.

SUGGESTION SYSTEMS

As a nation of independent free thinkers, there are some among us who function better as individuals than as group members. Their input may require individual recognition, as well. For such people, a suggestion system is a natural.

Can a suggestion system coexist with quality circles? Yes. A suggestion system, when properly administered, is just one more effective method of harvesting ideas.

The key to success in a suggestion system is organization and administration. Your quality improvement process steering group is an ideal group to set forth the ground rules. It gives them ownership of the system, determines who is eligible, establishes the chain of command for evaluation and approval, and provides the tracking system necessary to make certain that suggestions are moving and duplication is avoided.

Of equal importance is the determination of how you intend to stimulate participation by recognition and rewards. Avoid appealing to avarice and keep

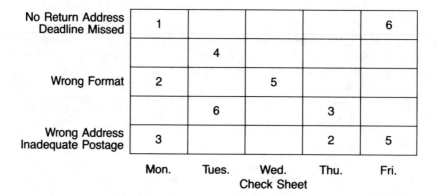

	Mon.	Tues.	Wed.	Thu.	Fri.
No Return Address / Deadline Missed	1				6
		4			
Wrong Format	2		5		
		6		3	
Wrong Address / Inadequate Postage	3			2	5

Check Sheet

	Material Correct
	Drawings Correct
	Gages on Hand

Check List

Figure 10-4

rewards modest. Recognition though, should be sky-high. Big-money incentives can become a nightmare of legal and financial problems you never imagined, but merchandise, privilege, and modest cash prizes can generate enthusiasm and participation. Bear in mind, employes are being paid for their efforts, and you don't want to divert their attention from that fact.

Sloppy or indifferent administration has killed many suggestion systems. Processing that takes six months to a year, rejection because of envy or threat to the status quo, failure to investigate poorly understood suggestions — all of these can cause suggestion systems to fall flat. The temptation to belittle suggestions is another thing that will completely kill a suggestion system. Evaluation of suggestions and notification to donors should take place within 30 days. An aggressively administered and publicized system with visibility given to implementation will do more to stimulate participation than you ever dreamed of.

STATISTICAL PROCESS CONTROL

Statistical process control through use of control charts is a recognized approach to assuring control of manufacturing processes. In 1950, W. Edwards Deming revealed this technique (developed by Walter A. Shewhart of Western Electric in the early 1920s) to Japan's top industrial management. He predicted that if they implemented process control, the world would beat a path to their door within five years. What prophetic words!

Can it assist you in reducing scrap, rework, and repair? Absolutely. Statistical process control, to some, smacks of a black art. Actually, it is only the application of data to monitor whether or not a manufacturing process is within acceptable limits.

We live in a world of variables. It's statistically impossible to achieve exact repeatability in any mechanical function. There are too many unavoidable variables in any manufacturing process. We can live with a *degree* of variability. Thus, specs are written with a plus or minus tolerance.

Statistical process control says that, as long as we can set upper and lower critical limits that accommodate the tolerance specified, we can produce acceptable products. The smaller the variation between these limits, the better. By gathering, averaging, and plotting data during the process, we can determine when we begin to exceed the limits and take corrective action. It may be that our measurements are askew or our machines need adjusting. Thus, we save the agony and cost of scrapping our material or investing time to rework or repair the item.

Characteristics of Distribution Curves

In order to understand the visual display of data variation, it is essential to define the basic nomenclature. The arithmetic mean of observations, values, or what have you, is called the *average*. The average is derived by dividing the sum of observations by the number of observations. It is designated by $\bar{X}$; thus the expression "X-bar." The *median* is the middlemost value and is calculated by arranging values in ascending order and dividing the frequency distribution into two equal parts: one equal part above and one equal part below the median. When the number of values is odd, the median will be an integer. When the number of values is even, an average of the two median numbers will give you the distribution median. The *mode* represents the value that occurs most frequently.

In a normal distribution curve — where 64.26% of the data falls within ± 1 sigma from the mean, 95.45% falls within ± 2 sigma, and 99.73% falls within ± 3 sigma of the mean or average — plotting of this data will attribute to the formation of a perfect bell-shaped curve as represented in Figure 10-5.

Control Charts

X-bar and R charts, sometimes called average and range charts, are statistical control charts and are illustrated by Figure 10-6. X-bar and R charts indicate the average of a scale of measurements, with R indicating the range or difference between highest and lowest in a sample. X-bar and R charts give the operator an indication of when the process is out of control. By checking first the data, then the set-up, the operator can determine what is necessary to bring it back into statistical control.

P-charts — another type of statistical control chart — require no measurements, only a count of the number of pieces that have like or unacceptable characteristics. These attribute measurements are expressed as defective percentage of a lot. Lot may be specified as the work of a specific operator or shift, or units that have like characteristics (i.e., voltage, finish, weight, etc.). It is another technique to determine where and why your process is out of control.

Histograms and Pareto Analysis

Histograms are another visually meaningful manner of plotting data. For example, by plotting the quantity vs. time on a bar graph, you will achieve a visual representation of the normal distribution of the data.

Vilfreto Pareto was an Italian economist and sociologist remembered by most for the analysis which bears his name. He suggested that, by grouping items of greatest quantity or importance on the left side of a bar graph and arranging items of lesser quantity or importance in descending order to the right, it is possible to make a rapid visual comparison of data displayed. A cumulative line can be added to demonstrate visually the value of each bar as an increment of the total (see Figure 10-7).

CHARACTERIZING DISTRIBUTION

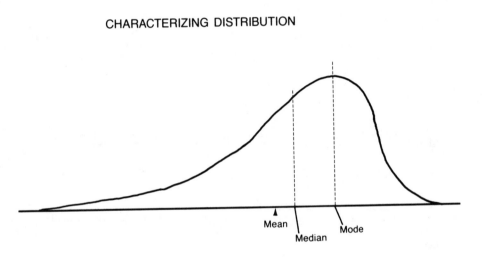

Mean:	Point of balance, 1st moment about zero.
Median:	Divides area in half.
Mode:	Point where f(y) is maximum.

Figure 10-5

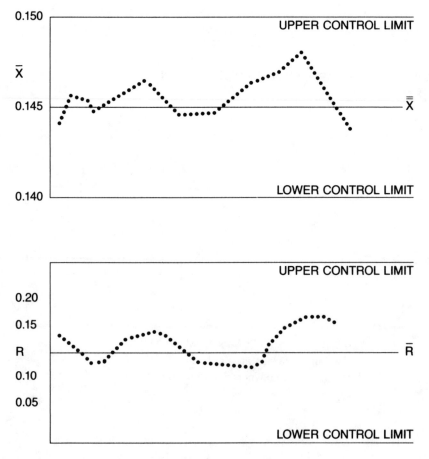

Shewhart Control Charts

Figure 10-6

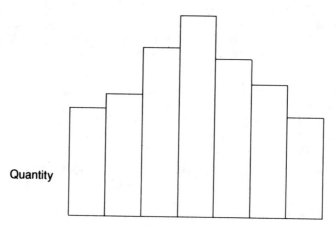

Quantity

Time

Histogram

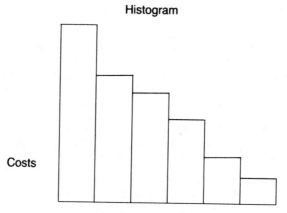

Costs

Unacceptable parts

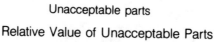

Relative Value of Unacceptable Parts

Pareto Chart

Figure 10-7

Pareto charts can be used to graphically display time, money, people, products, or whatever you desire. By stratification, they can be used to determine where sheer numerical size is dominant, or if other elements such as total number of product defects by line, by shift, by process, or by value more readily identify where effort will provide the most payback. Through use of Pareto analysis, hidden problems can be readily discerned.

Joseph M. Juran made Pareto's 80/20 theory famous by labeling it "the vital few vs. the trivial many"[1] (e.g., "In marketing, 20% of the sales personnel . . . account for over 80% of the sales. . . . In quality control, the bulk of the field failures, downtime, shop scrap, rework, sorting, and other quality costs are traceable to a vital few workers, machines, processes, etc.").

The "stem and leaf" histogram, the brainchild of John W. Tukey, not only gives you a graphic display of the amplitude of the data, but also the live numerical data. A further variation of the stem and leaf chart includes a reference to time so that *all* of the numerical data can be presented graphically (see Figure 10-8).

FLOW CHARTS

A flow chart is an analytical tool used to help determine the most logical path in determining a process in manufacturing or the sequence to take in unraveling a problem. It assists you in not only visualizing what needs to be done, but also helps you communicate that process to others. In essence, it is a pictorial representation of all the steps in a process, which helps the mind to more readily comprehend.

Potential trouble areas and omissions stand out starkly when committed to a flow chart. Comparison of an independently constructed flow chart with a chart describing a current process can quickly identify a weak spot in the process.

Flow charting uses standard symbols to indicate the type of process being performed. Figure 10-9 gives an example of these symbols and application.

VALUE ANALYSIS AND ENGINEERING

Lawrence Miles, father of value analysis and engineering, states, "The constant and accelerating flow of new ideas, new processes, new products, and new materials can, when properly applied, aid in establishing desired customer values at a lower cost. This leads to the conclusion that, when a product is designed, tooled, and on the market, it is already advancing to becoming obsolete."[2]

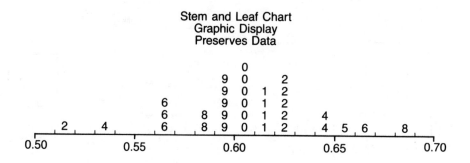

Stem and Leaf Chart
Graphic Display
Preserves Data

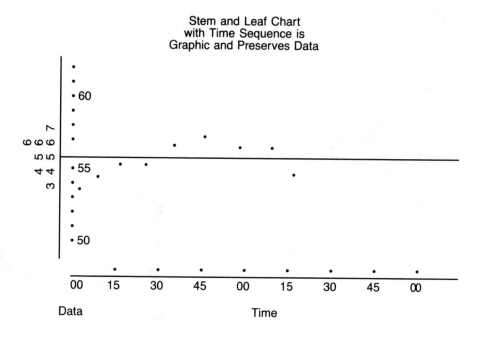

Stem and Leaf Chart
with Time Sequence is
Graphic and Preserves Data

Data

Time

Figure 10-8

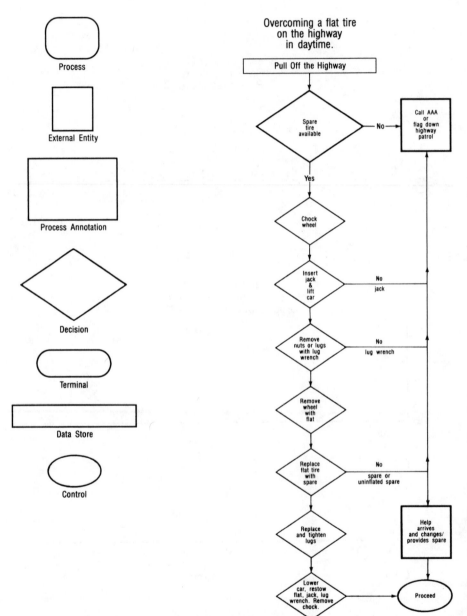

Figure 10-9

"Value" means a fair return on investment, and the customer defines "fair." Value has nothing to do with being the most expensive of its kind. Value arises from worth being equal to or exceeding the price paid. Worth, in turn, may arise from an item's usefulness — its ability to perform a function to the customer's satisfaction.

Satisfaction depends on reliability. An automobile that starts 99% of the time is not considered by its owner to be reliable if it doesn't start when he's taking his in-labor wife to the hospital.

Another element of value is longevity. Is the warranty a prediction of the date of product failure? If so, the customer will interpret breakdown as part of the manufacturer's plan. If planned failure *is* part of the manufacturer's plan, then the manufacturer doesn't understand value.

Look at value as a fraction. Price is the denominator of the fraction; longevity, reliability, style, and all other factors that contribute to customer satisfaction combine to yield the numerator.

Value analysis is of particular value in determining how to achieve maximum value for a product or process. A logical first step in the value analysis process is to determine just who your customer is. Determine what you make or do for him or her (what satisfactions you provide) and determine if you provide this service or product at the lowest possible price.

Bill Domings, the value analysis chief of the Paul Revere Insurance Companies, says that any process that has not undergone a change in 24 months has probably fallen behind the power curve. The environment-changing technology of this century doesn't allow dormancy.[3]

Value can be increased by honestly questioning everything you do. Not only is it important that you do things the most efficient way, but you must question whether you are doing the *right things*. Perhaps you're only doing what you'd like to do or what you're told to do.

Value analysis, judiciously done, can produce 35 to 40% savings and improved quality. It takes time, however, and if management is not prepared to allow time for workshops, expectations will never be fulfilled.

Purpose of Value Analysis

There are essentially six phases of a value analysis undertaking. First, determine what is to be examined, who is to be involved, the amount of time to achieve the undertaking, and who will coordinate it. This plan must be communicated to all involved.

Step two is an examination of the status quo. This is a serious event that determines what is being done, by whom, and why. Does it need to be done at all, and, if so, is it being done correctly? Now, look at the organization doing it. Could someone else do it more efficiently? Could it be combined with someone else's duties?

There can be no sacred cows during this exercise. The facilitator who leads the inquiry must look into even the most sensitive areas. For this reason, it is often judicious to engage an outside consultant who enjoys the trust of clients and has established the integrity of his or her capability.

Step three is the creative phase where the group performing the function brainstorms to see how the function could be done better. The sky's the limit during the brainstorming session. Criticism and evaluation are not allowed during this phase.

Step four is a natural follow-on — it's the examination and evaluation phase during which ideas with promise are sorted from those that are unworkable, too costly, or unreasonable. "Promising" ideas are those likely to reduce costs or improve the product or process. A cost reduction that reduces the process value is an unacceptable trade-off, just as is a change that improves neither effectiveness nor efficiency. A cost analysis is essential to determine what savings can be achieved.

Step five involves developing a recommendation for management's consideration. It must be clear, concise, and data based. As in quality circle recommendations, it should be verified to assure acceptability. As top manager, you are obliged to consider it thoughtfully and expeditiously to show your good faith in this process. Your approval may be given without giving audience to the recommenders. An audience, however, will serve as a very positive stimulation to the group, which may have worked from six to eight weeks on the recommendation.

Step six — implementation of the recommendation, follow-up, and monitoring to ensure it achieves the desired purpose — is all important.

A word of caution: Value analysis will help you to achieve the most if you make clear at the outset that no workers will lose their jobs. Retraining or transfer must be assured if you are to achieve maximum effectiveness. You may well question, if the purpose is to improve efficiency, how can one realize any gain if the payroll remains the same? The answer is simply that productivity will be gained and your present functions will be expanded. Normal attrition will do the rest.

Value engineering is simply an organized approach to identifying consumer expectations while a product's in the concept and design phases. How can these be met at the lowest cost? There must be an exhaustive study of what the product is expected to do, how long it is expected to last, the degree of reliability expected, and the maximum competitive cost. As price decreases with no corresponding decrease in function, reliability, or longevity, value is increased. This collection of data requires input from quality, purchasing, design, manufacturing, and marketing, and, when it's time to act on the data — to begin moving the product to market — those teams must function as one to meet the customers' expectations.

Value engineering looks not only at the functional technology of the product, but also at the materials that best fit the product, the tooling required, and the production and test sequences need to bring this product to the market on time and at cost. Value engineering questions every step of the design and development phases of new products, and basically uses the same sequences used in value analysis of a process.

VERIFICATION

The final step in any approach to assuring quality is the verification phase. As top manager, this is one of the first questions to ask when your quality circle or small group activity comes to you with managerial presentation: Has the validity of the problem they are presenting to you been verified?

Has the cause been established and verified through use on an Ishikawa diagram? How about the solution? Has the circle run a test that verifies the solution as being valid from performance and cost standpoints? Has it investigated and presented a cost-effective trade-off for the equipment or procedure being replaced? All answers should be data based.

Elevating problem solving to its rightful position on the manufacturing, engineering, or purchasing floor is one of the smartest single actions a manager can make.

KEEPING YOUR FINGER ON THE PULSE

The eight problem-solving approaches discussed are not new. They all have the seeds of success, depending on how actively management is involved. Support is not enough; participation is essential. Part of that participation requires keeping your finger on the program's pulse and being ready to act when the pulse gets weak, for none of these approaches will effectively run indefinitely. Checks and fine tuning, or even radical changes, can keep enthusiasm alive and efforts productive.

A change of leadership from time to time will do wonders. Keep your eye cocked for wind shifts; otherwise, you may suddenly find your ship adrift or capsized. As the skipper, your responsibility is to see that this does not happen.

Footnotes

1. J.M. Juran, editor, *Quality Control Handbook*, 3rd ed. (New York: McGraw-Hill, 1979) p. 2-16.

2. Remarks by Bill Domings of the Paul Revere Insurance Companies at value analysis course to Textron, Inc., Leesburg, Va., 7 July 1986.

3. Lawrence D. Miles, *Techniques of Value Analysis and Engineering*, 2nd ed. (New York: McGraw-Hill, 1972), p. 13.

CHAPTER 11

SO YOU WANT TO ESTABLISH A QUALITY IMPROVEMENT PROCESS?

How do you go about putting your organization on a quality course? The answer is not simple. It requires management involvement and the dedication of resources adequate to the task. It is an ongoing endeavor that involves people, and people are complex.

Following are 15 items that are extremely important in structuring a quality improvement process (QIP). They contain the rudiments of a plan of action guaranteed to give you positive results.

Step 1: Management Involvement.

Management involvement is where it all begins. Management must be physically as well as intellectually involved. The head person, the chief executive officer, the president or the chairman of the board, or the president of a division, has to be very firmly committed, dedicated, and involved in the entire process or the attempt to institute a quality improvement process will fail.

Employes have become very cautious of "new" corporate strategies. They've seen them come and go. They've seen management lose interest in them when significant results do not immediately occur. Consequently, many employes are cautious about embracing new programs. The best way to prove your sincerity is to involve yourself personally in the undertaking. Your staff and your employes will be the ones who implement the process, but *you* must keep your finger on the pulse, *you* must be visible during the implementation phase, and *you* must be the one to whom people are accountable for making this a successful venture. If you aren't interested in such roles, read no further.

Step 2: QIP Steering Committee.

If you want to take the plunge, your first step is to find a group of positive-thinking key personnel and other interested and involved employes to make up your QIP steering committee. Who should belong? Certainly your department or division vice presidents must be members. At least one member should be a representative of hourly employes, and a quality circle facilitator should be a member of this group.

If you can talk a union leader (where applicable) into joining the effort, you have a definite advantage over organizations in which the union decides to remain aloof. To sell a union representative, preferably a leader, on the concepts that the results of the effort will (1) improve employes' quality of work life, (2) enhance the competitive standing of the company (which will ensure the longevity of employes' tenure through improved market share), and (3) provide employes a better basis for increased remuneration by virtue of increased profit.

While the membership of this committee might not be totally voluntary, the majority of members should be volunteers. This will help to ensure enthusiasm and stamina for the long-range process you're about to launch.

Charter

Having determined the membership of the group, you should briefly describe the charter under which you desire the group to operate. The purpose of the charter is to determine how many and which of the elements of a QIP plan — outlined in following pages — they feel are necessary to improve the performance of their company. A word of warning: Don't encourage them to bite off more than they can chew! An incremental implementation will give you a good payback. Putting too much on their plate at one time will only invite disaster. However, the group should be encouraged to make a long-range plan that will eventually tackle all of the features contained in the QIP. Along with the decision on the initial project, a plan of action and milestones should be devised to indicate when and by whom the goals will be implemented. This will provide a degree of measurement.

The QIP steering committee should report directly to you, the top manager. It should be encouraged to meet once a month to hear reports from action officers who have been given the responsibility for implementing various tasks. The steering group's primary job, after it's hammered out an all-encompassing QIP, is to monitor the progress of the endeavor.

A very important member of the steering group is your quality circle facilitator. This, of course, assumes that you plan to implement quality circles — perhaps the most important initial factor in assuring your employes that you're serious about a QIP. (More about circles in Step 4.)

Step 3: Quality Policy.

While companies have policies for sick leave, vacation, retirement, hiring, pay, and promotion, incredibly enough, very few have a quality policy. What does a quality policy do? Very simply, it sets forth the standards and definition of what we mean by the word "quality." In addition, it establishes accountability for delivery of a quality product or service.

The quality policy statement need not be long, but it must be clear, concise, and comprehensive — something that can be provided to every employe with a reasonable assurance that he or she will understand what it means. Some goals set forth by a quality policy might be:

• To provide customers with products or services which meet or exceed their expectations.

• To provide employes with a desirable work environment — competitive remuneration and satisfying personal challenge.

• To provide stockholders with a competitive rate of return on investment and an image of competence and long-term stability.

To achieve these goals, you will need a high level of dedication from all employes and suppliers. Everyone must resolve to perform all aspects of his or her tasks as completely and thoroughly as he or she knows how, and to seek to improve all aspects of the organization for everyone's mutual benefit. The president or general manager of the company or division should sign that policy. It should be printed in a form that can be tucked in employes' pockets for ready reference, so no one will have an excuse for not following it.

A policy poster might state, "Quality is doing the right thing, doing it the right way, doing it right the first time, and doing it on time." Those four elements leave little room for misunderstanding what is meant by a quality policy.

This quality policy is hammered out by the steering group and then given to you, the top person, for approval and signature. Give the group a few guidelines on what you'd like to have included, but basically, the policy should be the work of the steering group.

Step 4: Quality Circles.

As was stated earlier, quality circles can be one of the most vital elements of your QIP. They involve participative management in its most effective form.

Shop around for a good program and make certain that the person or firm who will do the briefing and subsequent training really understands what quality circles are about and is completely competent. The Quality Circle Institute, located in Red Bluff, Calif., has one of the soundest plans for implementing the concept of any vendor in the business.

After briefing your steering group, if you and the group feel that circles are the way to go, your next step is to choose facilitators. The facilitators should be people who feel at ease before a group and can effectively communicate. They should have the respect of their peers and should be enthusiastic about quality circles. Otherwise, your quality circles may never get off the ground.

The facilitator is the person who trains your quality circle leaders and monitors them as they go through the training process with their quality circles. After training is completed, the facilitator will be the person who occasionally sits in on the quality circles to monitor their progress and to serve as a back-up for circle leaders. (Facilitators also try to field questions for which leaders don't have sound answers.)

In small organizations, it is recommended that there be at least one facilitator for 50 people. Regardless of whether or not you're going to implement them incrementally, this represents a good facilitator-to-circle ratio. In larger organizations — 500 to 10,000 employes — one facilitator can serve up to eight circles.

When the scope of quality circles within an organization has been determined, then the number of facilitators to accommodate the undertaking and the amount of training material necessary can be determined. Circle size should be no smaller than three and no larger than 15. Eight to 12 is an ideal size.

The facilitators herein described are people who have full-time jobs with the company and who perform circle service only as a part-time effort. Part-time facilitators are recommended because they can continue their primary duties and thus maintain a more balanced profile. The facilitators will report to the steering group on quality circle activities and will be a part of the deliberations on the QIP.

The facilitator normally receives three and one-half to four and one-half days of training in order to understand group dynamics and engineered problem solving. After the training is received, the facilitators' responsibility will be to train each of the quality circle leaders in their duties and techniques for interaction with members of the circles. If the facilitators are trained out of house, the training material will be furnished. However, if training is done in-house, then materials similar to those used to train the leaders should be procured. The training of leaders is normally a day shorter than the training of facilitators.

Before a facilitator is trained, the steering group should have made some kind of decision about the scope of quality circles within the organization.

While most quality circles experts indicate that the decision to join should be voluntary, there are pros and cons for voluntary and involuntary participation.

Voluntary participation allows everyone to make up his or her own mind, and thus, they'll be better suited to operate in the quality circles environment. If participation is involuntary, everyone has an opportunity to be introduced to the concept, which will make for a nonexclusionary type of atmosphere — the feeling that, if quality circles are good for one group of people, why should they not indeed be good for all hands? This latter argument seems logical.

After both facilitators and leaders are trained, the normal procedure is to have an information meeting for implementation. It will discuss the purpose of quality circles, the degree of training members will receive, the benefits to members, and the benefits to the company. If it is to be a voluntary undertaking, people should be allowed, after some thought, to indicate whether they wish to become members of circles. If it is going to be an involuntary effort, then this implementation information serves to break the ice for employes.

While facilitator and leader training is done on three and one-half and four and one-half consecutive days, training for circles themselves is usually a matter of one-hour lessons each week for six to eight weeks, depending on the scope of circles training desired. The Quality Circle Institute has an eight-meeting training course that ranges from an information overview of problem solving and problem prevention, to the final session, which concerns pointers for management presentation.

As soon as leaders are trained, implementation of the quality circles concept should begin. The training generates tremendous interest and enthusiasm in leaders, and the sooner you can take advantage of that momentum, the better off you are.

The facilitator's function, after having completed training of leaders, is one of an overseer and a mentor. He or she becomes your command sensor to determine how well quality circles are doing and when it will be necessary to assist the leaders in directing or in revitalizing the circles. Usually, however, when the facilitator attends meetings, he or she should sit quietly as an observer, responding only when invited to do so by the leaders.

Step 5: Recognition System.

There are many different ways of recognizing the accomplishments of your employes. Many managers feel that pay is the primary recognition, and some employers feel that it's the only one that's necessary. While salary scales are certainly a basic means of recognition, people like to be stimulated by personal acknowledgment from the boss. This can take the form of a pat on the back, a kind word as you walk around the plant, letters from top management, quality designations on the person's jacket or working garb, or plant-wide publicity that gives public recognition. All of these cost very little and can be very effective in establishing a quality culture among your people.

Social functions, too — picnics, potlucks, or company dinners — can be effective recognitions of people who make outstanding contributions to quality productivity or other areas of endeavor.

Some companies believe that cash prizes or gifts are the things that stimulate people to greater accomplishments. Many times, an agreement with a local merchant for gift certificates can have a very stimulating effect on employes' enthusiasm for the quality process.

A fourth type of award recognizes the quality team as a *whole*, with some monetary reward based on the savings that have accrued as a result of suggestions implemented. This can be in the form of individual cash awards to each member of the circle or one cash award for the entire group, which can be used for a celebration, athletic equipment, or anything that the circle can enjoy collectively.

The choice of recognition is up to you. There should be a gradation for various achievements, but a recognition program is definitely one that will earn big dividends for the quality culture you're trying to install.

Step 6: Process Control — A Systems Approach.

Process Capability

Of prime importance is *knowing* the capabilities of your manufacturing process or, put another way, the measured, built-in reproducibility of the product turned out by the process. Understanding if specification tolerances can be achieved, what production rates it will support, plus maintenance requirements necessary to hold tolerances — these are process capabilities that must be statistically derived.

There can be no question about process control's superiority to end-item inspection. The latter separates the good from the bad — hopefully — and ensures that the product will be to the customer's liking. However, it does not help reduce the cost of nonconformance, which is generated through scrap, rework, repair, warranty costs, and customer dissatisfaction. Scrap, rework, and repair are only the tip of the cost of nonconformance iceberg. Statistical process control, when applied to all vital dimensions, will assure that operators understand when a process is going out of control and future parts that are produced will have to be reworked or scrapped.

Before a statistical process control procedure is initiated in the plant, explain its purpose to the operators. When the use of control charts is mandated without any explanation or training, you'll find a tremendous amount of resistance, and the installation of the process will be a lengthy and costly one. Controlling the process from concept to delivery is an important aspect of any QIP.

Computer Software

The introduction of computers into industrial use in 1978 provided an entirely new dimension to quality. While CNC equipment has expanded man's capability to replicate processes with greater accuracy, no CNC machine is better than the software that controls it. While some feel that the computer has made people somewhat obsolete in the quality equation, bear in mind that it is the men and women who write and debug the program that are ultimately responsible for this "magic." A program is no better than the programmer's understanding of the process — whether it be drilling, machining, grinding, polishing, plating, hardening, tempering, extruding, and what have you — and the machine by which it is to be accomplished.

Just as it can produce spec-perfect parts, a computer program can just as easily produce defective parts if poorly executed. All depends on the quality of your software and its implementation and maintenance. What steps have *you* taken to provide your software development and maintenance personnel with a quality improvement process?

Step 7: Vendor Control Program.

Since most large companies now are assemblers or integrators, it's essential that the parts assembled — even if they are from subcontractors that furnish parts — will meet the specifications of the ultimate customer. When a vendor is being considered to provide components, a thorough QIP audit should be made of its facilities, procedures, and systems so you will be sure the product you receive is one that will be on time and to specification. If the vendor has a good quality assurance process, it's certainly reasonable to consider certification and to accept the product as a result of receiving inspection sampling or even a no-inspection dock-to-stock acceptance.

If the vendor has no quality assurance system, you might be well advised — at least initially — to do a source inspection or a near 100% receiving inspection. The source inspection, while a little more expensive, can provide certain benefits. It avoids delay in shipping time before you find out which parts are unusable. If there is an effective assurance system, an occasional spot check is generally adequate to ensure the acceptability of the parts. In the final analysis, the vendor must be encouraged to institute an effective quality assurance system.

A vendor rating system is sometimes desirable in order to show vendors how they rate as far as your company's quality standards are concerned. It is always beneficial to have vendor briefings *before* the vendor begins supplying a part so that it will understand the end item to which it is supplying parts and the operating conditions to which it will be subjected.

I recall observing an incident where a vendor was producing turbine blades for a very high-speed gas turbine. The operators, all of whom were very dedicated workers, had no idea of the high speed and temperatures to which these blades would be subjected. They, therefore, failed to recognize the fact that tolerances had to be precise. The prime contractor began a program of having personnel take orientation flights in the aircraft in which their turbine blades were used, and the lesson was learned very quickly.

Annual briefings for vendors, calling them all together to reiterate the quality desired and any changes that might have occurred in the end-product, are another excellent way to ensure good communications and good relations.

In addition to vendor briefings, a vendor recognition system is an excellent way to stimulate vendors. Consider an annual contest to determine who is the best vendor. Make certain that it's based on performance and that it gets the publicity it deserves. Anything that causes vendors to feel membership on your team is definitely to your advantage, and any methods that can be used to engender such identification are certainly worthwhile.

Step 8: Customer Concern.

The reason service or manufacturing industries exist is, of course, the customer. Often this aspect of business somewhat fades from view as "the customer" becomes an impersonal name on an order blank instead of a real, live identity whose success is dependent on how well you fulfill his expectations of the product or the service you're supplying. This being the case, it is essential that there be a customer barometer that measures exactly how the customer — whether he's a prime contractor or an end-user — feels about your product. In either case, its positive perception of your performance is necessary for your continued prosperity.

How do we implement such a barometer? One way is through use of questionnaires, which require as little writing as possible on the part of the customer and which are couched in such a manner as to make the customer feel that you are truly interested in its best interests and that completion of the questionnaire will get results.

A simpler way, if you have fewer customers, is a phone survey, which gets right to the customer and allows him to comment very candidly on the product without a great deal of effort on his own part. This seldom is as comprehensive as a questionnaire, although it may be much more candid. But, once again, it is an effective method.

A third approach to determining how the customers feel about your product or service is, of course, personal contact — having your marketing or engineering people sit down with customers to determine how they feel about what it is that you're providing.

Another tool is a feedback slip accompanying each product or lot delivered. This works particularly well if it has postage attached. Then it's just a matter of simply making checkmarks or a few written lines and dropping the form in the mail, reducing the amount of effort the customer is required to exert in order to give feedback.

Step 9: Recruiting Program.

Your most important element in any QIP is people. So very often, we hire them without a great deal of thought or research into their experience, background, or, particularly, their attitude.

Marv Runyon, president of Nissan America in Smyrna, Tenn., says one of the most important criteria for hiring a person to work at Nissan is how the prospective employe feels about the company. The motivation to join Nissan has to be for more than the pay or more than just a job. The criteria used in assessing the future employe is focused on determining whether the person really wants to become affiliated with Nissan because it is a premier auto and truck manufacturing company.

The recruiting and screening program should determine how qualified the person is for the job, and this can be discerned from recommendations and from experience. It is certainly an important phase in determining the value to the company of the applicant. Educational background, while important, should be secondary to the person's potential for becoming a contributing employe of the company. A good balance between education, experience, and attitude will assure that the potential the person has is realized. Being too quick to employ can sometimes end up in additional recruiting and training costs. The degree to which one can reduce turnover certainly adds to a firm's quality quotient.

Step 10: Training Program.

A well-organized, formal, documented training program is another key to the success of your QIP. The assumption that little training is necessary if the person is qualified when applying for the job can lead to headaches later. Each company has slightly different ways of doing things, and a good orientation course and an observation period will pay big dividends later. Welders, solderers, and critical assemblers should be certified, and periodic requalifications conducted to assure competency.

There should be someone who bears the responsibility for writing the program and training accomplishments should be documented. The training program should have its own separate budget for the simple reason that, otherwise, when there is a drop in the economy, the first budget to be cut will usually be training. If the training program is controlled by someone from top management, such cuts can be avoided.

Training can be accomplished either in-house or through the use of outside consultants. If an outside consultant is used, investigate his or her qualifications thoroughly. Bear in mind also that outside trainers do not understand your organization or needs as well as an in-house trainer/consultant. In-house trainers, no less than outsiders, must be well qualified to ensure that your product will be one you and your customers can live with.

Step 11: Suggestion Systems.

Many people are fulfilled by being a part of a successful team, but some prefer individual contribution and recognition. They feel quite capable of developing a suggestion completely by themselves and submitting it to management. And they, in turn, would like to get full credit for it. While the synergistic effect of quality circles cannot be disputed, neither can it be denied that there are some people who are not team players and who would prefer to present an individual contribution to the improvement of quality. By having a suggestion system as well as quality teams or circles, you can harvest all of the potential ideas that have been lurking in the minds of employes for years but of which we have not been taking advantage.

A word of warning, though. Don't start a suggestion system unless you're serious about going through with it. The possibility of a six-, eight-, or twelve-month lag between the time an idea is proposed and the time feedback is given is one that will kill a suggestion system.

Timely feedback requires an organization to review the suggestions and refer them to experts (industrial engineers, design engineers, etc.). They will determine if a suggestion is feasible and how much it will benefit the company when effected. There must be a feedback system that responds to the individual within two weeks, even if it's nothing more than interim reply or an acknowledgment that the suggestion is now in the system. Take no more than six weeks to complete the review and inform the person who proposed the suggestion of the results, so he or she understands that it is not languishing in someone's "too-hard" basket.

How do you pay for suggestions? The are as many different ways of rewarding good suggestions as there are people who have them. One is to give a percentage of first-year savings recovered from implementation of a suggestion.

A caution regarding suggestion systems is that one must consider legal ramifications. Make certain you don't set yourself up for a lawsuit for having disregarded a suggestion or having used one without any compensation. Have your legal department study this, and make certain that your suggestion system is well protected.

The key to any successful suggestion system, though, is to be responsive and fair to those who offer input. There is a great deal to be gained from such systems, and having quality circles in no way diminishes the power of this additional harvesting tool.

Step 12: Inventory Control (MRP).

Inventory represents money. It represents both capital in the amount of material or components tied up in inventory, and it represents money in the space needed to store it. It also requires money for the people who are going to be handling the inventory. The smaller the inventory, the greater the profit, and the more efficient the operation.

Naturally, it's important that the inventory is the kind which can be used to support the production schedule. This entails good planning, which falls in the hands of your information specialist, or whoever is responsible for your materials requirement plan (MRP). It also depends a great deal on the vendors who will be supplying this inventory.

For example, one of Sony's plant in Japan has vendors who arrive at their loading dock every one and one-half hours. Essentially, vendors are the warehouses that store Sony's components for its color TVs and VCRs (which roll off the line at a rate of one every six seconds).

Inventory control and good MRP require a close liaison between your MRP czar, manufacturing, and purchasing. As long as you have a functional integration of these people, there should be no question about the effectiveness of your inventory system.

Step 13: Organizing for Quality.

While organization will not necessarily give you quality, it should definitely be a part of your QIP. The idea that your quality department is solely responsible for quality is one of the first myths essential to quash. Quality is an all-hands effort, which, if supported and participated in by everyone from the top banana to the janitorial crew, will produce a product or service that can only please the customer. My personal observation is that when the vice president of quality reports directly to top management, he or she achieves the prestige of peer status with other vice presidents (engineering, purchasing, manufacturing, finance, etc.). However, when the head of quality is a director or manager — particularly if the position reports directly to manufacturing or engineering — he or she tends to be less influential and visible.

Functional integration of quality, design, and manufacturing will assure a quicker start-up and a minimum of engineering change orders after production has begun. A clear understanding of manufacturing capabilities by engineering will assure that you have a producible product; and, with quality riding herd to make certain that the process can be controlled, you'll find few rejects coming out at the end of the line.

Purchasing, engineering, and manufacturing vice presidents must also be functionally integrated. If purchasing's philosophy is dictated by low bid, manufacturing will often find itself trying to assemble junk. By the same token, if there isn't effective integration between engineering and purchasing, it will be impossible for purchasing to really understand what is needed in order to assure that the parameters of the design have been well met.

The third area of functional integration must be among design, marketing, and manufacturing. If marketing sells a product that is far ahead of the state of the art (particularly if it's done within a time constraint that precludes a serious study and test period), again, you're faced with potential failure. Marketing should understand the capabilities of design and manufacturing before beginning to sell a product.

The fourth functional interface should be among human resources, engineering, and manufacturing. What kinds of people are necessary in order to meet the requirements of the business you're in? What types of engineers do you need? What kind of experience should they have? What kind of production people are essential in order to be able to run the plant? All of these are items that must be known by your human resource people, since they do the recruiting and hiring.

The fifth interface should be among administration, finance, public affairs, and management. What kind of image is desired for the company — a low profile or a high profile? Top management must make the decision on this and assure that the image is well understood within advertising, finance, and public affairs.

The organization, while it's not the "be all and end all" of quality, certainly contributes to any QIP.

Step 14: The Cost of Nonconformance.

Comedian Bob Burns, the bazooka humorist, used to feature a skit in which he explained why the leak in the roof never got fixed. "When it's raining, can't; when it ain't, don't need to." Failure to document the cost of nonconformance will predict, in much the same manner, continued nonconformance costs and all that that implies to your earnings, to the reputation of your product, and to the morale of your personnel.

The value of determining the cost of nonconformance is indisputable. It makes the difference between a business with sustained market competitiveness and one that will limp along and eventually go under. Being able to identify where your hemorrhage of profit will occur as a result of scrap, rework, repair, warranty costs, lost contracts, legal suits, etc., is very important in structuring a program to stop this outflow of profit.

By first brainstorming the possible sources of nonconformance (this can be an activity for your QIP steering committee), one can then determine areas worth documenting. Once this is done, the scope of such a cost can be determined.

Nonconformance costs manifest themselves in design changes that cause production changes, scrap, rework, and repair. Excess inventory to meet production schedules is another dimension of nonconformance costs. Contract delivery delays can result in penalities, loss of credibility, or contract cancellation. Post-manufacturing costs should likewise not be omitted from your calculations. These include field reps, warranty, repair and replacement costs, and, most costly of all, your firm's reputation and repeat business.

Consider just the cost of rework. In cost of labor alone, it represents three times the investment of doing it right the first time: First-time-through cost, rework cost (which will often be greater than the original cost), and the cost of not producing an additional item in the rework time slot (since time is being used for rework). Consider also the moral of your rework line. Can these individuals be very happy redoing work they or their associates have messed up?

Without a clear and concise method of documenting your cost of nonconformance, you will never know the magnitude of earnings going down the drain or the location of the leak. This cost should be calculated as a percentage of direct labor costs.

The cost of nonconformance, when properly calculated, will always get top management's attention, since money is a language most readily understood. It also will gain the attention of workers who can recognize their loss of competitiveness in the marketplace. When there's a profit-sharing plan, advertising the cost of nonconformance can be an *exceedingly* effective way to gain the attention of the workers.

Defects are not free. Industry caclulations are that nonconformance costs run from 10 to 40% of direct labor costs. Once sources are identified and a corrective action program developed, a monitoring procedure to determine the efficacy of the corrective action system should ensure that you have a trend going in the right direction. It's important that the trend be charted so everyone will be able to understand what their efforts have contributed to the improvement of productivity.

Achievement of a quality culture is entirely possible, but only to the extent you know the nature and roots of your quality problems.

Step 15: Accountability.

As in any system that is worth its salt, it's absolutely essential that there be a degree of accountability for the process. This means that people must be assigned to implement each step. They must have an infrastructure that allows them to appropriately control the process; and, with that in place, they can be held accountable for actions. The QIP steering committee, of course, must also make it understood that action officers will be accountable for seeing that the program moves in the right direction, and, when problems are encountered, they are reported at an appropriate level for review and correction. Without accountability, very little can be realized from any QIP.

SUMMARY

What is apparent after reading through the 15 steps involved in setting up a quality improvement process is that a successful QIP focuses on three essential elements of quality.

The first is *quality of management.* As I said at the beginning of this chapter, unless the top person is interested in more than survival and achieving a sustained competitive market advantage, talk of a QIP is futile. Deming and Juran agree that the majority of errors negatively impacting quality and productivity can be laid at management's door; ergo, let's concentrate first on straightening out that aspect.

Chapter nine is devoted to the second essential element of a QIP, *quality of work life.* A quality of work life program looks at hiring the appropriate people, giving them necessary training to develop a confident and proper attitude towards work, providing them with adequate tools to do a first-rate job and facilities that give them good reason to be proud and identify with the company, and then supporting them with the kind of recognition that says *"you are* our most important asset and we *do* appreciate your best efforts."

The third element is *quality of performance.* This is where the rubber meets the road, where customers become aware of just how important they are to a company's sustained competitive market advantage.

These three elements are covered thoroughly in the 15 steps I have outlined. May you have great success in applying them.

CHAPTER 12

THREE ELEMENTS OF A NATIONAL STRATEGY

Our national strategy for regaining a reputation for quality and competitiveness has three main elements: We must improve the quality of management; we must look at the quality of work life and learn to treat our employes, and not our stockholders, as second in importance to our customers; and, we must focus on quality of performance — training, procedures, and products.

QUALITY OF MANAGEMENT

Knowing What Your Business Is

First, decide what business you want to be in. Is it the business you *are* in? Mergers, buy-outs, and diversification have put many companies into businesses about which their managements know little or nothing. Once you know what business you're in, and if that business is one you've actively chosen and have appropriate skills to pursue, you're ready for step two.

Knowing Where Your Business Is

Is your business solely bottom-line oriented, or is it a business that considers the customer to be the most important aspect of business?

Is your business focused on its product to the degree that you investigate your competitors to see what their related products are doing? It is not enough to know what your product is doing. Know also what your competitor is doing to get ahead of you.

Is your business market-oriented? Is it capable of discerning market desires and filling needs as unlikely as Hula Hoops, Trivial Pursuit, Pet Rocks, discotheques, and other fads that earn their creators large sums of money. These are classic examples of being market-oriented.

QUALITY: THE BALL IN YOUR COURT

Is your business proportionate to the market share you're attempting to capture, or are you going after more of the market than you can or want to satisfy? Are you purposely limiting output to create an artificial shortage and keep price and profits high? You may be inviting a hungry competitor to undercut you.

Are you change sensitive? Can you instinctively discern changes in market needs? Or, if not blessed with such insight, do you keep your ear to the ground to detect the sounds of market change? Have you "trip-wire alarmed" the product to tell you when the market is saturated and is looking for something different?

Who is responsible for strategic planning in your business? Is it solely in the hands of your planning department, or do you insist on this important aspect being a team effort?

Are your people developing positive attitudes regarding quality? Is it more than a catch phrase? Do they really understand what quality can mean to the market (and to themselves)?

Do you have methods of harvesting the potential bumper crop of ideas germinating in the heads of employes? Are employes motivated to communicate ideas to management?

And, when the going gets tough, what's your reaction? Do you hang tight and scout the market and competition to see what must be done to gain wind advantage once again?

Accountability

Accountability appears to be another lost or diluted tenet in today's business world. Managers who, through inattention, incompetence, or indifference to the essence of management, put a business in the red, create unfavorable media attention, or are at loggerheads with a labor union, are seldom held accountable. Instead, they are laterally transferred or kicked upstairs. They're rarely fired.

While Harry Truman was manager of the world's biggest business — the United States — he had on his desk a small sign that read, "The buck stops here." This should be on your desks, too, managers. Stop looking for a scapegoat and start providing leadership.

A chief executive's most valuable contribution to the future of his company is the motivation he provides subordinates — providing it requires his involvement, his being in on details when necessary, and his maintaining visibility with employes. Concomitant with that is the need to recognize individuals, shifts, sections, and divisions for their special achievements. The morale-lifting potential of such action is without equal.

QUALITY OF WORK LIFE
AND THE SIX "P'S"

Let's look at six "P's" that impact quality of work life — people, policy, procedures, practice, persistence, and patience.

Policy

Do you have a quality policy? Is it well understood? Does it say what you want to happen and assign responsibility for making it happen? Do you and your management team abide by the policy, or, when push comes to shove, do you ship despite the protests of your quality people? Missed schedules are preferable to receiving defective material. Make your quality policy inviolate and your people will soon believe you are serious about this thing called quality.

Procedures

Do your people on the assembly bench or production line know how to make that product right the first time? Even an airline pilot who has thousands of hours behind him runs through a detailed checkoff list prior to takeoff and landing simply because the airline cannot survive without guaranteeing passenger safety.

So it goes with written procedures. Yes, an assembler may have performed a given operation many times, but see that that procedure is in front of him and he understands it. Establish procedures in accounting, design, and engineering — acceptable to each discipline — as an insurance and standardization safety net. Concomitantly, ensure provisions for the necessary training, equipment, and facilities to support those quality producing procedures.

Practice

Periodic audits, including "management by walking around," will determine whether or not your policies and procedures are being practiced. Unpracticed, they lead to "followship anarchy." A true saying is that an unenforced law or policy is worse than no law or policy at all. As a matter of fact, it becomes a measure of management's lack of concern for detail. To be effective, the policy and procedures must be continually enforced. If they aren't worth enforcement, they should be dropped or changed.

Persistence

Many battles are lost because we weaken and decide to change course, not realizing we're close to victory. So often, the resistance to change is nothing more than a test of wills, to see just how serious we are about the change. Persistence, far more often than intelligence, is the difference between success and failure of a program or career.

Patience

You decide this business of a quality culture may have some merit. You give your quality VP the go-ahead to design a quality improvement process. You participate in its implementation. You are disappointed that others don't see the value in it. You become disenchanted with your short-sighted management team or first-line supervisors who are offering passive resistance. Your union spokesmen criticize your efforts as being phony, transient, or another example of management trying to squeeze labor.

Don't lose your perspective or your patience. Don't allow yourself to be shouted at or stared down. Don't get angry or resort to their tactics. Be patient and bear in mind that you and they have different motives for work and different problems with which to cope.

People

Finally, people are at the root of the success of any undertaking, whether it be the production of quality and competitive automobiles, or fighting a war. Despite the wonders of technology, people have the last word on quality. They have the power to make or break your quality campaign. Give them motivating leadership and they will follow you. Listen to them, treat them as individuals, and keep them informed about what the company is doing. Involve and train your employes to use proven problem-solving methods by implementing quality circles and reap the benefits of their very fertile minds. Bear in mind that they are the real experts of what is necessary to achieve consistent quality on the production floor.

QUALITY OF PERFORMANCE

Quality of performance must be addressed by management, and the most logical area is to include it in both your strategic and business operating plans. I suggest five measurable goals that will lead to success: 1. *Attainment* — Appraisal of individual, measurable quality goals; 2. *Training* — Amount and quality accomplished; 3. *Reduction in your company's cost of nonconformance* — Essential to first establish a base line; 4. *Degree to which vendor product acceptance has improved* — Also requires base line measurement; and, 5. *Sensitivity to customer* — Measured by reduction in returns, rework, customer complaints, and lost business.

Let's look at these goals a bit more closely.

Quality Goals

First, look at quality goals and objectives. Are they a requirement for all your supervisory personnel and management teams, as well as yourself? If not, issue a policy that henceforth will require such.

Don't adopt quality slogans that imply goals that cannot be measured like "Improve Quality in 1986" or "Enhance Quality of Work Life for Employes in My Division." Richard Simmons, CEO of Allegheny Ludlum Steel Corp., says, "If you can't measure it, you can't manage it." An unmeasurable goal or objective has little motivational power for the subject personnel. Quality goals must be measurable in dollars, time, or materials saved.

To Train or Not to Train

In one of my many plant tours in 1983, the president of a valve manufacturing company was showing me (as his customer's rep) through his plant. I picked up one of the components and put a go/no-go gage on it. It didn't go. I noted several others that were no-go, but in the go side of the bin. The irate president, who was observing my actions, queried a supervisor about the worker's qualifications and was told that the man who had produced the pieces was a new hire who had passed himself off as a journeyman machinist. On the strength of that, and without having his credentials or skills checked, the new hire had been put to work.

Lack of training very often is where customer dissatisfaction begins. Can you afford to jeopardize your customer's loyalty in this manner? Bear in mind Deming's statement: "Your customer is the most important part of your production line."

Basics of a Training Program

Training is perhaps the master key to quality products, and it contributes significantly to quality of life (from the job satisfactions and security inherent in knowing what we are doing).

QUALITY: THE BALL IN YOUR COURT

The level of training required for any given employe should be established in employment interviews. Unless you're prepared for significant investment and effort, screen out applicants with reading or math deficiencies. An apprentice program or adult education is more suitable for people with these educationa deficiencies.

As described in chapter eight, training can be formal or on the job — the forme being far preferable, since it allows the trainee full concentration without the tension a production environment represents. Any training should be structurec and implemented by a competent supervisor (and any training should include a rationale for total effort — a view of the quality end product and the employe's part in producing it).

Once your new employe is competent and can meet your quality standards, put him to work under supervision until he feels at home on the shop or plant floor. Catch the new worker's mistakes or unacceptable work habits early, before they become ingrained and before the worker comes to consider them acceptable to your standard of quality. Don't wait to bring them up in his quarterly or annual performance appraisal.

Skill and Quality Training

During most of the past four decades, permissiveness, "do your own thing," and "get away with what you can" have governed our management and other work force personnel. Progressive education, with its modern math, has produced generations who lack reading, writing, and analytical skills. If we are to regain a quality-oriented work force, we must educate all involved in what we mean by quality, dedication, and commitment.

This reeducation should take the top-down approach. The sooner top management understands the value of quality training, the more likely it will be able to provide resources for the training of middle management supervisors and operators. Top down also signals the importance of training.

Quality training is an area where this nation has considerable expertise. Juran, Deming, Feigenbaum, and Hunter are internationally known and their philosophies are widely used and acclaimed. All four have been instrumental in setting up effective training programs that have borne rich fruits in Japan.

The choice of bottom up or top down is not nearly as important as ensuring that training encompasses the scope of total quality control. To focus on one area being the most important one isn't nearly as beneficial.

CHAPTER 12: THREE ELEMENTS OF A NATIONAL STRATEGY

SQC — A Must

Statistical quality control (SQC) is a must for all hands. Komatsu issues each new worker a pocket-sized book that contains not only the company quality policy, but a summarized description of SQC. The accompanying training program begins with a week of studying X-bar and R charts, histograms, scatter and cause-and-effect diagrams, and Pareto analysis. Workers are steeped in the truth that quality is neither inevitable nor unachievable. They learn to determine if a process is in or out of control. They learn sampling as a means of making inspection economically feasible.

Too often, managers who have come up the routes of accounting, law, or business administration feel uncomfortable when quality professionals talk about SQC or statistical process control (SPC). There is a need — *not* for a top manager to become expert in these areas, but that he or she understands what SPC is, what it does, what it can mean to success, and why it is important. Managers don't assume that they must be as technically competent as their workers before they go out on the floor, and they should adopt the same attitude about dealing with quality. But managers *should* know the *right* questions to ask and understand the answers that they receive.

Nonconformance is Costly

Reducing nonconformance is another key tactic. It's staggering to realize that 60 to 90% of the expense of nonconformance could and should be going to the bottom line. To determine this cost, add up component costs: scrap, rework (times two or three to account for man-hours spent duplicating operations instead of building new products), repair, costs of administering a material review board, warranty work, engineering changes and drawings, complaint service time, test, reinspection, retest, source or receiving inspection costs, and fixed preventive costs. This latter item may take a long time to reduce, but, to impress you and your managers with the total cost of nonconformance, add it in. Cost of nonconformance is important, and anything important should be measured. (A detailed formula for alleviating the cost on nonconformance appears in Appendix B.)

A 1982 U.S. Consumer Affairs survey has some interesting facts about what nonconformance does to your customer: 96% of one's unhappy customers never complain to the producer. Of those who do complain, 91% never buy again from the offending company. Each complainer shares his or her unhappiness with at *least* nine to 20 people. Sobering thoughts.

So, now that you have assessed nonconformance, how will you eliminate it? The corrective action plan should be a joint effort of design, engineering (if it is a separate organization), manufacturing, and quality. In a service organization, it must be attacked by marketing and operations at a minimum. And, of course, it's essential that you be briefed on the plan if you didn't participate in forming it, and that you receive periodic reports on its progress. You must be prepared to see the cost trend rise for at least the first year as your colleagues continue to identify new areas of nonconformance costs. Once that base line has been established, expect there to be a downward trend. Be cautious, however, about setting ambitious goals or you will find yourself victimized by number crunchers who can make numbers represent anything they think the boss wants.

Your Vendors

Vendors can make or break a prime contractor's quality. The vendor's component may cause your product to fail, but you will get full credit for the failure. It will be *your* customer who fails to renew the contract with you.

In Japan, primes do amazing things to and with vendors. Essentially, vendors maintain the primes' inventories. They deliver on time, at cost, and free of deficiencies. And, of course, that is exactly what they're supposed to do.

Do your vendors consistently deliver on time, at cost, and defect free? If not, what can you do about it? If a vendor is the only one bidding on a contract, firing him will mean an interruption of production. You can't ignore the vendor's mistakes, for that will encourage perpetuation of the nonconformance.

Invite the vendor to visit your plant to see how his contribution helps or hinders the success of your product. Stage a "Quality Day" and invite *all* your vendors. Give them a walk-through and a series of briefings by design, engineering, manufacturing, quality, marketing, and, yes, if possible, provide a couple of your big customers to explain what quality means to them. Point out the needless cost of receiving inspection — a duplication of the vendor's preshipment efforts.

Do a thorough audit of your vendors' statistical process control before you sign a contract with them. Periodic audits will warn you when they begin to slip. The importance of documentation and audit has been covered previously. It is an extremely vital function in any industry.

A more drastic step is to do 100% receiving inspection and charge the vendors for the cost of this and any other time spent in rework, return, production stoppage, etc. This will most certainly get their attention.

Knowing the Customer

As the U.S. Consumer Affairs Committee's survey points out, only about 4% of your customers *tell* you when they are unhappy. The rest just cancel their business with you.

Consider your own actions as a consumer — you buy a toaster that, after three months of use, burns the toast. It sets off your smoke alarm that you don't know how to silence. Do you send the toaster back? The guarantee requires that you return the unit to the factory or nearest authorized repair service, neither of which are convenient, and besides, the toaster was on sale and only cost $15.75. You "deep six" it and buy a new one. The same brand? Hardly. The manufacturer of that toaster has lost a customer and doesn't even know why.

If you as a producer are interested in knowing what your customers think about your product, ask them. Send out questionnaires or send marketing reps out to sit down with them to discuss the merits and demerits of your product. Too much trouble? Afraid you might rock the boat and cause customers to wonder about the reasons for your concern? Don't worry. Customers can't help but admire your interest in their welfare, and that kind of good will is money in the bank.

SOLVING QUALITY PROBLEMS

The venerated dean of U.S. quality, W. Edwards Deming, has formulated a celebrated wheel which reads, "Plan, do, check, act." I have developed another wheel to help identify and defuse problems. I call it my "Eight 'Ates" in dealing with quality problems.

The "Eight 'Ates"

Your sales drop, your competitor prospers. You're forced to lay off personnel. Complaints about late deliveries, defective merchandise, or incomplete or wrong shipments stream into your office. You have a quality problem. You *investigate*. Your first reaction must be to determine the scope, nature, and area of the problem.

Have all the bits and pieces of information at hand before you evaluate the seriousness of the problem and the resources you'll need to solve it. Is the customer or vendor the problem, or is it company related? If the latter, is it a matter of lack of expertise, training, equipment, poor design, or indifferent management? Can the problem be handled with on-board talent, with outside expertise, or will it require both?

Having evaluated the problem, *premeditate*. Structure a plan for solving the problem. Focus on the root cause, not just symptoms. Bandaids only assure that the problem will recur. Naturally, the plan will depend on resources and commitment.

Next, *integrate* plan and action. Assign responsibility for implementation, establish milestones, achievement dates, and flesh-and-blood individual accountability. Plans without action are like plants without roots.

Remember, quality is an all-hands project, so *participate*. If the troops don't feel their leader is taking lead in quality, they'll conclude that quality isn't a real concern.

Now, *motivate* employes to identify and address the causes and costs of nonconformance. Stress how much more satisfying as well as profitable it is to do it right the first time. The company's profitability and employes' job longevity depend on recapturing pride in workmanship.

Motivate customers to feed back dissatisfaction in a specific and timely manner that can help you give them a better product or service. If you are a customer, announce to your suppliers that you intend to recoup not only the price paid for the defective goods, but that you are also going to tack on a surcharge for your time and effort in ascertaining the defects and returning the defective goods. Feedback helps suppliers understand that shoddy, nonconforming parts will not be acceptable.

Interrogate. Is your corrective action plan working? If not, why not? Has someone dropped his end of the load? Is there any misunderstanding about what was to be done and who was to do it? Perhaps, on observation and reflection, you will discover the plan did not really reach the root of the problem.

Enter the eighth 'ate: *Eradicate.* Pride is a costly luxury. Don't let it stand in the way of eradicating the deficiencies in a corrective action plan that "didn't work" and moving on from there. You must reevaluate and continue in a logical sequence until the root is identified and the flaw in your quality program is eliminated. Only then can you feel successful.

A FINAL WORD

The three most critical areas of effort in introducing a quality culture to an organization are *attitude, discipline,* and *resources,* and, of these, the most critical is attitude.

Attitude

"Attitude is, without question, the most critical change that must occur in order to achieve a quality culture."

Your subordinates have seen management go off on many tangents, only to grow tired of the lack of interest or success and drop the program. Too often, they look on top management as "the Christmas help" — here today and gone tomorrow. Sharing a common understanding of the meaning of quality and performance standards is an essential beginning.

CHAPTER 12: THREE ELEMENTS OF A NATIONAL STRATEGY

Creating ownership of quality goals among your employes will do more to make the quality culture a reality than almost anything else you can do. Team membership — greatly enhanced by quality circles — will do wonders to change attitudes. In addition, a few recognized successes will inspire, motivate, and also change attitudes. Education, example, and recognition are the most effective approaches to changing attitudes regarding the importance of each person's contribution to quality.

Discipline

"Discipline is an essential element in exacting efficiency and effectiveness."

It took courage and self-discipline to carve a nation out of the wilderness our forefathers found when they settled this country. Weather, Indians, long distances from Mother England, and Mother England herself were all obstacles to conquer. However, they understood that the essential element in exacting efficiency and effectiveness in creating this new nation under God was discipline. They demonstrated it time after time as they overcame human enemies and natural obstacles. They recognized that the essence of self-discipline was in accepting that what each individual did was essential to success.

And so it is with discipline. Each person must have a self-discipline that says "What *I* do is essential to quality!" If every person doesn't exercise the self-discipline of recognizing his or her individual essentiality to quality, it will not occur. This self-discipline must prevail from concept to completion. I'm talking about process-control discipline that runs the gamut from concept to billing, a system discipline that considers customers, employes, and vendors all vital to the success of quality.

Resources

"An inescapable top management responsibility: resources."

One of the basic premises I have regarding a quality improvement process which is destined to be successful in changing a culture is management involvement because management controls all resources. Improvement in equipment, capital improvement of facilities, enhancement of manufacturing systems such as CNC or FMS — all must have management approval. I've observed that management is often waiting for business to improve before the company updates to become competitive. Business will improve only to the degree that companies believe and are willing to invest to make themselves more competitive.

QUALITY: THE BALL IN YOUR COURT

Resources are the *sine qua non* of a quality culture. They enable or disable the quality process, and *you* are the controller. You are the financially responsible individual who is (or should be) accountable for disbursement of company funds. Resources are indeed an inescapable top management responsibility.

And time is your most valuable resource. It is spread thin by visits to divisions, board meetings, routine administration, travel, marketing, customer stroking, etc., but, if your quality improvement process is to be successful, it requires your time, your participation, your involvement.

You must also allocate financial resources, training, equipment, and expertise to support quality product or service delivery. It takes guts to spend money when your peers and bosses have doubts that there will be any significant return, but guts and talent win ball games and wars, so press on.

When your quality improvement program accomplishes its goals, it is vital to reward all those who made it possible. If the pie has grown bigger and those who made it happen don't get a share, your quality improvement process will die. Your union will proclaim it was just as they expected — labor makes the wealth, but management gets all the glory and benefits.

Is it possible to create a quality culture in your plant or organization? It definitely is, providing you are committed to making it happen.

The quality ball is in *your* court.

EPILOGUE

When this nation took on Spain to assist Cuba in attaining its independence, President William McKinley needed to send a message to General Garcia, head of the revolutionary forces in Cuba. The exact whereabouts of General Garcia were unknown, except that he was somewhere in the jungles of Cuba.

Someone suggested sending a young army lieutenant named Andrew Summers Rowan. Lieutenant Rowan was summoned and given an oilskin pouch containing a message to Garcia. His instructions, put plainly and simply, were to deliver the pouch to General Garcia. The where, how, and when to deliver the message were left up to Rowan, who was put ashore on Cuba from an open boat. Disappearing into the jungle, he traversed the hostile jungle for three weeks and reappeared, his mission completed.

While I would be immodest to compare myself to Lieutenant — and later Colonel — Rowan, within the pages of this book is also a message to Garcia. More accurately put, this message is to *all* the General Garcias who lead our manufacturing and service industries. To these General Garcias I say, "Take heed."

The message is clear and has been delivered. The enemy has been identified: nonconformance to the customer's desires and requirements. The issue is *quality*.

Your challenge is to press home and *implement change*, so that the message in this book will be as effective as the message to General Garcia from President McKinley via Lieutenant Rowan. Good luck!

QUALITY: THE BALL IN YOUR COURT

APPENDIX A

TYPES OF INDUSTRIES
VISITED DURING 1981-83

Product Breakdown	%
Space/aircraft	10
Level 1/subsafe/nuclear power	10
Heavy machinery (e.g., tanks)	10
A/C components	7
Truck/car manufacturing	7
Weapons systems (radar/sonar, etc.)	5
Missiles	5
Electronics (chip)	5
Electronics (precision instruments)	5
Miscellaneous	5
Clothing, textile, and shoes	4
Ammunition	4
Electrical (general)	4
Communications equipment	3
Light machine manufacturing	3
Ordinance	2
A/C overhaul	2
Metal manufacturing	2
Shipbuilding	2
A/C parts (distributor)	2
Training simulator	1
A/C manufacturing	.04
Petroleum	.04
Robotics	.04
Computer	.03
Camera	.03
Optical	.02

QUALITY: THE BALL IN YOUR COURT

APPENDIX B

COMPUTING THE COST OF
NONCONFORMANCE (NCN)

Cost of Nonconformance

$$\$NCC = \frac{{}^*\$\ S\ +\ WO\ +\ RR_1\ +\ RR_2\ +\ CA\ +\ IE\ +\ PMC}{\$B}$$

NCC = Nonconformance Cost

S   = Scrap

WO = Work Omission

RR_1 = Rework and Repair

RR_2 = Reinspection and Retest

CA   = Corrective Action

IE   = Inventory Excess

PMC = Post-manufacturing Cost

B   = Base (For trend monitoring, this should be in constant dollars.)

*   = All labor costs to have burden applied.

Scrap:

   • Replacement cost of item (product, part, material, tool, software, etc.) at point of loss consisting of:

147

• Labor (manufacturing, quality, planning, scheduling, etc.) plus

• Cost of productivity lost due to rescheduling or resequencing factory and equipment (cost of additional equipment or tooling setups, cost of additional factory and equipment carried due to known or expected nonconformances, cost of nonavailability of factory and equipment for normal production, other costs of doing work out of sequence) plus

• Cost of capital associated with loss of productivity.

Work Omissions:

• Reprocessing cost due to nonconformance to requirements because of missed or partially completed operations or activities.

• Cost of productivity lost due to rescheduling or resequencing factory and equipment effort (cost of additional equipment or tooling setups, cost of additional factory and equipment carried due to known or expected nonconformances, nonavailability of factory and equipment for normal production, other costs of performing work out of sequence).

• Cost of capital associated with loss of productivity.

Rework and Repair:

• Cost of total manufacturing labor expended to reduce severity of or eliminate nonconformances.

• Labor cost of planners or schedulers and others involved.

• Cost of work stations added in manufacturing sequence to perform rework due to low process yields.

• Internal cost for correcting supplier deficiencies.

• Cost of rework effort included in standards for task accomplishment.

• Cost of additional material required.

• Cost of activities as above due to engineering changes (other than customer-required design changes) or technical data errors.

• Cost for correcting spares and spares provisioning data.

• Expenses and travel required.

• Cost of productivity lost due to rescheduling or resequencing factory and equipment effort (cost of additional equipment or tooling setups, cost of nonavailability of factory and equipment for normal production, cost of additional factory and equipment carried due to known or expected nonconformances, cost of out-of-sequence work, etc.).

- Cost of overtime expended.

Reinspection/Retest:

- Cost of quality assurance or control efforts resulting from other events (scrap, work omissions, rework, repair, etc.).

- Cost of required support personnel such as test equipment operators.

- Cost of additional screening or inspection effort to detect or remove same or similar conditions.

- Cost of any manufacturing labor that operates inspection points as prescreening activity.

- Cost of overtime expended.

Corrective Action:

- Administrative cost of operating material review activity and corrective action systems including labor cost of personnel (quality, engineering, manufacturing, clerical, other).

- Cost of failure investigation and analysis of both hardware and software (including embedded software) nonconformances including time of source quality, engineering, and purchasing representatives where applicable.

- Engineering time required to correct design or drawing errors including software design and programming errors.

- Labor and administrative cost of processing engineering and data changes due to design or human error through the configuration management activity.

- Labor and administrative cost of correcting or revising manufacturing and inspection procedures or instructions.

- Internal labor cost (purchasing, manufacturing, quality, engineering, other) to obtain replacement vendor parts or material.

- Costs of correcting defective numerical control tapes.

- Costs of waivers and deviations, including all processing costs.

Inventory Excess:

• Cost of additional stock carried due to known or expected nonconforming parts or material (both purchased and manufactured in advance of needs).

• Cost of capital charge associated with excess stock.

• Cost of expedited deliveries to meet artificially created, earlier-than-necessary need dates.

Post-manufacturing Cost:

• Warranty cost of returned products.

• Cost of field service effort in lieu of returns (labor, expenses, travel, etc.).

• Cost to retrofit nonconforming material.

• Cost of lost product utility/longevity/reliability/maintainability of "use-as-is" material.

• Software cost.

Base:

Total manufacturing direct labor dollars (including overhead).

Quality System:
Measure of Effectiveness

• Quality operations (cost as percent of total operating cost).

• Vendor component rejection rate (numerical as well as dollar value percent of total buy reduced to cost to remedy).

• Engineering design changes (those essential to producibility after initial submission for production).

• Number of Material Review Board actions, requests for deviation, and requests for waiver (each as a percentage of the number of different products produced).

• Scrap, rework, and repair as percent of total manufacturing costs.

• Returns (scrap, rework, other costs).

• Warranty action (cost to repair or replace).

APPENDIX C

QUALITY DEFINITIONS AND IMPLICATIONS FROM ANTIQUITY TO THE PRESENT

On quality, an ancient discipline:

"If a builder constructed a house, but did not make his work strong, with the result that the house which he built collapsed and caused the death of the owner of the house, the builder shall be put to death!"

> Article 234
> Code of Hammurabi
> Circa 1750 B.C.

On quality, as prescribed in antiquity:

"If a boatman calked a boat for a Siegnor and did not do the boat well with the result that the boat has sprung a leak in that very year, since it has developed a defect, the boatman shall dismantle that boat and strengthen it at his own expense."

> Article 234
> Code of Hammurabi
> Circa 1700 B.C.

During the time of Apostle Paul, quality was an issue:

". . . and this I pray, that your love may abound yet more and more in knowledge and in all judgment; that ye may approve things that are excellent; and that ye may be sincere and without approach til the day of Christ."

> Philippians 1:9-10

QUALITY: THE BALL IN YOUR COURT

On director's guidance:

"My philosophy on how we are to do our job? It is merely this: *we must be so thorough that the only way we will permit the delivery of any product of poor quality is to be overruled by someone who is authorized to accept that responsibility.* I am personally committed to this philosophy; I ask you to do no less; and I assure you of my support."*

> E.A. Grinstead
> Vice Admiral, SC, USN
> Director, DLA

QA Reporter NR 43 (Apr-May-June 1982).

On Britain's national campaign for quality:

"The government believes that *quality* is the business of every member of the work force, and particularly that of top management. Chief executives must take the lead and make quality a *personal* responsibility."

> Lord Cockfield
> Britain's Secretary of State
> for Trade

On the issues of quality and productivity:

". . . Following the example of our forebears, we need to rely on basics, yet dare to dream, always remembering that there is *no* substitute for quality. Excellence must never be compromised."

> President Ronald Reagan
> August 20, 1984

Quality Defined

"Quality is *everyone* trying to do a better job; make a better effort at whatever he is doing in order to improve his performance and improve Avco's performance for *our customers.* We are looking for everyone to think in terms of how *I* can do it differently, how can *I* do it better to achieve total performance, and because of this, we as individuals get better *job satisfaction* from doing so."

> Robert B. Bauman
> Chairman of the Board
> Avco Corporation

"Let there be *no doubt* that all of us mean what we say when we define quality for Avco as *defect-free* and *doing it right the first time*. There is nothing more important than achieving our *quality objective* and maintaining the drive required to *institutionalize* Avco's *Quality Culture*."

> Donald K. Farrar
> President and Chief
> Operating Officer
> Avco Corporation

"Quality control does not mean achieving perfection. It means the efficient production of the quality that the market expects."

> W. Edwards Deming
> Quality Consultant

"Quality is an achievable, measurable, profitable entity that can be installed once you have commitment and understanding and are prepared for hard work."

> Philip B. Crosby, Chairman
> Philip Crosby Associates

"Quality is an attitude and a personal commitment to excellence. Quality is also our strongest competitive weapon."

> Douglas D. Danforth, Chairman
> Westinghouse Electric
> Corporation

"Quality is our best assurance of customer allegiance, our strongest defense against foreign competition, and the only path to sustained growth and earnings."

> John F. Welch, Jr.
> Chief Executive Officer
> General Electric Company

"Also of considerable importance, in my judgment, is the sense of personal pride and esteem that grows out of a quality effort ..."

> L.W. Lehr, Chairman
> 3M Corporation

"As quality goes up, so does productivity. Consider the impact on overall levels of productivity — if everyone and every machine performed properly the first time, every time."

> William M. Conway, Chairman
> Nashua Corporation

QUALITY: THE BALL IN YOUR COURT

"Quality is what the customer perceives when he feels that a product meets his needs and lives up to his expectations."

W.R. Thurston
President and CEO
GenRad Corporation

Quality of Life

"Live neither in the past nor in the future, but let each day's work absorb all your interest, energy, and enthusiasm. The best preparation for tomorrow is to do today's work superbly well."

Sir William Osler

"Live one day at a time, and make it a masterpiece."

Anonymous

"It's a funny thing about life . . . if you refuse to accept anything but the best, you very often get it."

Somerset Maugham

Quality Quotables of the
Bottom-Line II Conference
(Washington, D.C.: 1 June 1983)

"High quality in weapons and military equipment will be possible only when the chief executive of the producing company has a strong personal commitment to it."

David Packard
Chairman of the Board
Hewlett-Packard Company

"Many industries have accepted as normal a 15% scrap rate for their products as compared with a scrap rate of 1% in Japan."

J.M. Juran, Chairman
Juran Institute

"Attitude is the critical issue."

> William J. Weisz
> Chief Operating Officer
> Motorola, Inc.

"The Navy should be more patient in not insisting on production of a weapon before it is ready. We need a working, reliable, mature system when it gets there."

> Admiral Sylvester Foley, USN
> CINC, US Pacific Fleet

"We have been deficient in defining what our requirements are."

> General P.X. Kelley, USMC
> Asst. Commandant

"The cost of correcting defects in weapons runs in the range of 10 to 30% of the cost of each weapon. This represents enormous waste — billions of dollars."

> Paul Thayer
> Deputy Secretary of Defense

QUALITY: THE BALL IN YOUR COURT

APPENDIX D

EXAMPLES OF QUALITY POLICY VERBAGE*

Perfection Quality Policy

The Perfection Company is dedicated to the manufacture of high-quality reliable products that meet the needs defined by our customers.

Achieving customer requirements, as defined by specifications, is the responsibility of all Perfection employes.

The BIG Q

Providing customers with what they want, when they want it, at the promised price.

Quality Policy

Our company policy is:

• To provide our customers with products and services that meet or exceed their expectations.

• To provide employes with a desirable work environment, competitive remuneration, and a satisfying personal challenge.

• To provide our stockholders with a competitive rate of return on investment and an image of competence and long-term stability.

*Note: All quality policy statements should be signed by the chief executive officer and distributed to all employes.

QUALITY: THE BALL IN YOUR COURT

To achieve these goals, we need a high level of dedication from *all* employes and suppliers to perform all aspects of their tasks as completely and as thorougly as they know how and to seek to improve all aspects of the organization for our mutual benefit.

XYZ Quality Policy

We, as XYZ employes, commit to designing, manufacturing, delivering, and quality products and services that meet or exceed our customers expectations.

APPENDIX E

SUGGESTED INDUSTRY SPONSORED INITIATIVES TO IMPROVE QUALITY

1. Explore increased application of statistics in the design stage of projects to determine probability of success in design-production transition.

2. Industries and trade associations endow a "Quality chair" at select business/engineering institutions.

3. Establish a task force of industry procurement contracting officers, project managers, and DCAS representatives to develop QA techniques for implementation in new product development phase.

4. Support the establishment of a "President's Quality Award" to be presented annually to those industries meeting an established criteria in areas of quality ranging from published policy to product excellence.

5. Establish within each industry quality goals and standards as a means of measuring quality improvement.

6. Organize joint industry/DOD committee to devise standard contract form to achieve greater uniformity of content and simplicity of understanding.

7. If your company has experienced a major improvement in product or service quality, volunteer to be a Harvard Business School case study so that other industries will have an opportunity to recognize the positive impact that quality can have on profit and productivity.

8. Top managers of companies with successful quality improvement programs can offer to conduct seminars at leading business schools on management's role in and responsibility for improving quality.

9. Company engineers and managers could become involved with local educational institutions to ensure the pertinence of courses being taught in the quality field by auditing school classes and curricula.

10. Give your top engineers a sabbatical to teach in a university setting so he or she can bring an undated understanding of production and quality problems to the attention of future engineers.

11. Develop an organization — comprised of industry, academe, scientific, engineering, and management communities — similar to the Union of Japanese Scientists and Engineers (JUSE) to solve quality problems. Publish results and establish training programs to ensure quality awareness and understanding from top down in the industrial and white-collar hierarchies.

12. Promote a quality leadership policy within industry that is oriented toward product reliability vs. warranty.

BIBLIOGRAPHY

Abegglen, James C., and George J. Stalk, Jr. *Kaisha: The Japanese Corporation.* New York: Basic Books, 1985.

ANSI/ASQC B1.1 (Guide for Quality Control Charts), B1.2 (Control Chart Method of Analyzing Data), B1.3 (Control Chart Method of Controlling Quality During Production). Milwaukee, Wis.: American Society for Quality Control, 1985.

Bradford, David L., and Allan R. Cohen. *Managing for Excellence.* New York: John Wiley & Sons, 1984.

Deming, W. Edwards. *Quality, Productivity, and Competitive Position.* New York: McGraw-Hill, 1982.

Drucker, Peter F. *Concept of the Corporation.* Boston, Mass.: Beacon Press, 1960.

Dunn, Robert, and Richard Ullman. *Quality Assurance for Computer Software.* Cambridge, Mass.: Massachusetts Institute of Technology, 1982.

Feigenbaum, Armand V. *Total Quality Control,* 3rd ed. New York: McGraw-Hill, 1983.

Fukuda, Ryuji. *Managerial Engineering.* Stamford, Conn.: Productivity, Inc., 1983.

Ishikawa, Kaoru. *Guide to Quality Control.* Trans. by the Asian Productivity Organization. Tokyo, Japan: Asian Productivity Organization, 1983.

Ishikawa. *What is Total Quality Control? The Japanese Way.* Trans. by David J. Lu. Englewood Cliffs, N.J.: Prentice-Hall, 1985.

Juran, J.M., and Frank M. Gryna, Jr. *Quality Planning and Analysis,* 2nd ed. New York: McGraw-Hill, 1980.

Miles, Lawrence D. *Techniques of Value Analysis and Engineering*, 2nd ed. New York: McGraw-Hill, 1972.

Miller, Lawrence. *American Spirit*. New York: Warner Books, 1984.

QC Circle Headquarters, Union of Japanese Scientists and Engineers, ed. *How to Operate QC Circle Activities*. Tokyo, Japan: JUSE, 1985.

Schaeffer, Francis A., and C. Everett Koop. *Whatever Happened to the Human Race?* Old Tappan, N.J.: Flemming H. Revell Co., 1979.

Western Electric Co. *Statistical Quality Control Handbook*, 2nd ed. Indianapolis, Ind.: AT&T, 1958.

INDEX

A

Accountability, 31, 84, 130, 132
Acton, Lord, 15
Advertising, and quality, 12
Allegheny Ludlum Steel Corp., 135
Allen, George, 35
American Productivity Center, 60
American Society for Quality Control, 60, 61
Anglo-American Council on Productivity, 61
Aoki, Mikio, 61, 62
Apprentice training, 5. *See also* Training
   in Europe, 48-49, 51
Attitude, impact of, on quality, 88-89, 140-41
Automation
   impact of, on quality, 6, 31, 43, 50
   in Japanese industry, 56-57
Automobile industry
   in Europe, 8
impact of quality standards on, 3-4, 8, 13
   in Japan, 3, 8, 63-64
   in United States, 3-4, 8, 13, 39, 63, 64
Avco Operations, Textron, Inc., 86
Average, 108
Average and range charts, 108

B

Balance of payments, impact of quality on, 2
Bauman, Robert B., 148
Blue-collar worker, and quality, 31-32
Bonus system
   in Japan, 55
   in Korea, 72, 73, 75

D

Daewoo Shipbuilding and Heavy Machinery (DSHM), 71-72
Dae-Yeu Tech College, 75
Danforth, Douglas D., 85, 149
Dassault, 49, 50-51
Datsun (Nissan), 3, 39
Defense Contract Administration Service, 28, 61
Defense Contract Administration Service Quality Assurance Representative (DCASQAR), 25, 28-29
Defense Industrial Plant Equipment Center, inventory of outdated machinery at, 37, 59
Defense industry. *See also* Military readiness
  characteristics of, 19-20
  impact of quality standards on, 2, 4
  inventory of outdated machinery at, 37, 59
Defense Logistics Agency (DLA)
  Bottom-Line Conferences, 35
  management of Industrial Plant Equipment program by, 59
Defoding, 49
Deming, W. Edwards, 11, 31-32, 54, 63, 64, 65, 81, 105, 135, 136, 139, 149
Deming Prize for quality, 53-54
  criteria for, 59-60
Design
  correlation of, with production, 13-14, 49
  and quality, 31
Detail
  attention to, 25-26
    in Japan, 55-56, 57
Directors
  choice of, in Japanese industry, 66
  responsibility of, for quality, 94
Discipline, and quality standards, 89-90, 141
Distribution curves, 105-108
Documentation
  of quality, in Europe, 48
  of scrap and rework, 5, 71-72, 74-75
Domings, Bill, 113
Drucker, Peter, 83
Dulles, John Foster, vi

Q

Testing programs, in Europe, 48
Texas Instruments, 14
Thayer, Paul, 2, 151
Thurston, W. R., 150
Tohoku Nitsuko Ltd., 94
Tokyo Juki, 66
"Too-short" contract requirements, 7-8
Toshiba Corporation, 13
Total quality control (TQC)
    in Japan, 56
    in Korea, 71
Toyota, 3, 20, 39, 64, 65
    joint venture with General Motors, 39
    and just-in-time inventory, 20, 69
Trading companies, in Japan, 59, 65
Training. *See also* Education
    apprentice, 5, 48-49, 51
    cross-skill, 81
    in Europe, 48-49, 51
    formal vs. on-the-job, 5-6
    in Japanese industry, 58, 59, 61, 81
    and nonconformance, 34
    on-the-job, 6
    role of, in quality program, 5-6, 17, 81, 125-26, 135-36
Truman, Harry S., 31, 132
Tukey, John W., 110

U

Unemployment, in Japan, 56-57
Union of Japanese Scientists and Engineers (JUSE). *See* JUSE (Union of
    Japanese Scientists and Engineers)
Unions
    in Europe, 47
    in Japan, 15, 16, 55
    in United States, 15-16, 70

V

Value analysis, 110-13
    purpose of, 113-14
Value engineering, 114-15

Y

Yamaoka, Takeo, 66, 68
Yamazaki MAZAK Co., Ltd., 12, 20
YHP, 56
Yoshida, Premier, vi

Z

Zero defects standard, 81, 82
  as goal, 17-18
  and Japanese industry, 65
  in Korean industry, 74-75
Zettlemeyer, 48-49

QUALITY: THE BALL IN YOUR COURT